The Helen Burns Poetry Anthology

This anthology is dedicated to the memory of

Helen Burns

who served on the Board of Directors of the
Academy of American Poets
from 1968 to 2000

Mrs. Burns worked tirelessly on behalf of American poetry. She was known for her annual poetry luncheons, huge affairs dedicated to the appreciation of poetry and attended by dignitaries from around the world. In the 1970s, she succeeded in convincing the U. S. Postmaster General's office that America should honor its best poets by featuring them on postage stamps; starting with Edgar Lee Masters in 1969, the series eventually included Emily Dickinson, Sidney Lanier, Robinson Jeffers, Robert Frost, Paul Laurence Dunbar, and T.S. Eliot. Mrs. Burns also produced a number of master classes on poets and poetry as part of the Washington Poetry Circle. The life of Helen Burns is a legacy of love, support, and advocacy of poets and poetry, and the Academy is grateful for her long involvement and generosity.

THE HELEN BURNS POETRY ANTHOLOGY

New Voices

from the ACADEMY OF AMERICAN POETS

University & College Prizes, Volume 9

edited by MARK DOTY

ACADEMY OF AMERICAN POETS | NEW YORK

Volume 9 includes poems that received an award from the Academy of American Poets College and University Prize program between 1999 and 2008.

Managing Editors: CJ Evans & Emily Hunt
Design: Billy Merrell

Printed in the United States of America
by McNaughton & Gunn, Saline, MI

ISBN: 978-0-615-31940-7

Academy of American Poets
584 Broadway, Suite 604
New York, NY 10012
www.poets.org

CONTENTS

2000

Introduction

The Academy of American Poets has sponsored its College Prizes for decades now, offering encouragement to perhaps three generations of younger poets. I was myself the recipient of one of these prizes, in 1971. I was a freshman at the University of Arizona, and I'd written a long and dreamily associative poem called "The Green House." I can't remember a whole lot about it save that I composed catalogues of the attributes of the house I was imagining, and that it was fervid and smoldering: "Now I am going to the green house, the house on the street of smoking pearls . . ." one of the lines ran. I was seventeen; that was the year that William Stafford read some poems of mine and said, "Well, I have a feeling these are poems in heaven, but they aren't really poems on earth yet." That was the kindest thing he could have said; he recognized a potentiality, a yearning in me, and suggested, in a gentle way, that I had some work to do.

It was later that year that Mark Strand chose my poem. I felt the good things that a prize makes a young poet feel: heartened, a little more brave, confirmed in the notion that the work Stafford had suggested I needed to do was worth it, that it might lead somewhere. My private scratchings and fumblings might become, if I could find ways to shape them, something that could speak to someone else.

Some version of that story has happened over and over again, though more accomplished poems than mine – many of them gathered here – have been recognized, and their writers given a bracing boost. The hundred bucks I won was very welcome, but it wasn't the money: a poet I admired held my words in his hand and said yes to them.

One thing evidenced, in this rich and varied collection, is the power of teaching. What happens when poets teach poets? I don't think you could say that they taught their students to love the art; there must have been an interest already there, a desire to make something durable and vital out of words, and at least a nascent faith that such a thing could be made, somehow, if one tried hard enough.

But certainly teachers of writing can help deepen their students' passion for the word. This happens in any number of ways. First off, a good teacher is a fountain of resources, able to locate those poets a student might profitably read. This is a kind of art in itself, trying to intuit what another person might love. Sometimes these recommendations are based on content, or on a formal affinity, but often it's a tone, a way of making meaning that seems to have some resonance with what the developing poet might be trying to do.

Of course a teacher can, and usually does, convey some principles of craft. But the truth is that these are nearly always provisional and contextual. What's right for a taut, spare evocation of feeling may feel more-or-less useless in an expansive, Whitmanic catalogue. And artists tend to respond to rules of any sort with a healthy defiance. My friend who gives her workshops a list of unusable words each year is, to put it directly, asking for it; who doesn't read such a list and start dreaming up possibilities?

I think myself that there are two essential things a teacher of poetry does. The first is to try describing a writer to himself or herself, as precisely as possible. "This is what I see you doing" seems to me one of the most powerful phrases we could employ, if simply because it is very hard to see one's own writing with any clarity, especially early on in the process. Such acts of description might address stylistic habits, lines, sentence making, habitual gestures, recurrent themes, or questions. A good description makes us feel known, which is an incredible gift; a less-successful one at least has the virtue of provoking our thinking: is that who I am, does that describe the poem I've written?

The second essential thing we do is be fellow citizens, fellow makers, and fellow lovers of the art. The characteristics of such a person are curiosity, an appropriate degree of bewilderment, humility in the face of the great dead, and the ability to take and to express pleasure. Allen Grossman describes the conversation of poetry as a feast around a table, or you might also think of it as sitting together beside a fire – a very old fire, one that goes on without us, yet is quite amenable to being tended.

This notion of poetry as a kind of transmission between the past and the present is powerfully stated in a poem by the late Jason Shinder, from his posthumous book *Stupid Hope*:

ETERNITY

A poem written three thousand years ago

about a man who walks among horses
grazing on a hill under the small stars

comes to life on a page in a book

and the woman reading the poem,
in the silence between the words,

in her kitchen, filled, with a gold, metallic light,

finds the experience of living in that moment
so clearly described as to make her feel finally known

by someone – And every time the poem is read,

no matter her situation or her age,
this is more or less what happens.

Jason's poem suggests to me that younger writers are somewhere along the way toward knowing themselves, in order that, in the long run, a reader might look into their work and likewise, feel "finally known / by someone." What could be better than that?

As long as there have been creative writing programs, somebody's been bashing them in print. This is an expression of a perennial fear of homogenization and commodification. Why anybody thinks young writers would be better off working at coffee bars or painting houses while practicing their craft alone is beyond me. It's a lot harder to find people to talk to about Muriel Rukeyser or Jack Spicer that way. I can't imagine a better alternative – at least for a part of one's life – than immersion in a community of like-minded souls, where the things you care about are crucial to others, and you can form friendships with people who want to argue with you, love what you do enough to criticize it, and can't wait to show you the amazing thing they've just read. In a country the size of this one, such people aren't always easy to find; the university connects us to other readers, brings us into conversation. The faux-populist notion that if we just got the academy out of the way, poetry would thrive naturally among a grateful people seems to me naive; the reality is probably that market forces would have buried it even more deeply than they already have.

If indeed writing programs ever homogenized writers, they are far less likely to do so now, when we have a national network of writers increasingly linked by the Web, by rapid reviewing, publication, and discussion. Back when I was lucky enough to have my poem chosen, news didn't travel quite as quickly nor esthetics intermingle with such promiscuous energy. In Tucson, I was more likely to read the poets my teachers liked and the work of my peers; I didn't know what was going on in Charlottesville or Missoula or the Lower East Side; now such knowledge would be pretty well inescapable.

As for commodification, well, poetry is likely to take care of that prospect all by itself. You can produce a book of poems and offer it for sale, but you cannot prevent anyone from memorizing a poem, reading it out loud to friends, copying it out and e-mailing it; you hope, in fact, that people *will* do those things. Art gets given away, again and again, which means it's worth everything and nothing. Is there a risk of selling out? Only in terms of censoring our own turbulent or difficult or unsettling material, out of a misguided desire to please, or perhaps in terms of following patterns of thinking and speaking that are already laid out for us.

I suspect the real resistance to writing programs lies in a failure to come to terms with a paradox. How can I teach you to do what I don't know how to do myself? I do not know, plainly, how to write your poems. No teacher does. A skillful person can show you how to solve an equation or how to speak Urdu, but no one but you knows how to write your poems, and if you are a young artist you don't know yet either. But you will; that's what those who sign on to the enterprise of teaching writing must believe. And that's what the lively, achieved work in this collection demonstrates.

Anna Journey, a graduate student at the University of Houston, served as an assistant editor – indeed a co-editor – with me on this collection. I'm grateful to her for her acute eye and close reading, as well as to Billy Merrell, CJ Evans, Emily Hunt, and the staff at the Academy of American Poets for their labor on behalf of the word.

– Mark Doty

FRANCISCO ARAGÓN

Jugglers

for my mother (1932 – 1997)

She and I on a bench eating prawns:
the first day of her fiftieth year and she points
at two street performers about to juggle
fire, and a distant summer morning

surfaces, afloat on the light wind blowing
off the bay – older sisters in the dark, hiding
as big brother parades around the house

his hands outstretched and clutching large candles
I'm on a search! he shouts,
marching from room to room

till he finds them huddling in a jungle
of clothes, his beacons flickering as flame-
hot wax begins to flow across his fingers . . .

while she is walking to Centro Adulto, her head brimming
with phrases: the words she needs to learn so she can quit
sewing, maybe land a job in a bank; and the sitter

arriving minutes late, finding us wet
and trying to save a coat, a shirt, a dress – it's
a small one: nothing the green hose

and frantic assembly-line of buckets
doesn't eventually douse, leaving walls and curtains
the color of coal – *¡Mira!*, she gasps

her left hand rapping my shoulder, still pointing with the right
as the torches,
from one juggler to the other,

begin to fly

WILLIAM S. BARNES

12/8 or Vice Versa

Either way it snowed.
Juniper berries and hail stones sleep together in God's bead box,
The creek overflowed.
Pine needles and fresh mud and yelling at the dog:
Get off the street! and strangers:
What's going on?

These are pearls, dry-land pearls –
like hummingbirds.

Skeet shooters at the lodge blow things up.
Clay pigeons die no matter what.
Like gravity getting out.
Red penstemon reminds me of Mt. Sopris
and Kathy Kuhn riding double bareback and tight
all wet and wanting in our sleeping bags
filling tin cans with wild flowers
the smell of pine
getting to the top and seeing nothing but air
and snow. Columbine.

The creek overflowed.
New silt splattered impressions like coins
like doll-silver hand-pressed coins
pads of tiny toes each walking – everything
bent with mud. The dog
whines, afraid of guns, afraid of winter.
The mountain pours out its extra –
garbage stuffed into the gauging station –
bits of blue glass –

It was also the circumstance of being inside the event that made unthinkable the very notion that a witness could exist.

There is language for this –
the raven speaks in currents of mud

        – capillary.

III. Water (My Daughter)

she thinks hard about vitamin d, calcium, condensation and the
importance of water. she thinks herself into existence and for the
first year will sleep between us, a local accumulation of cells,
bone transmitting light, a soft milk-tooth bluish-white. she's all
water except for where she's bone carved out by water, and the
boundaries where they happen to meet, their opposite bone
faces, the bony indeterminacy of ball meets socket. they and we
never roll onto her space. a body knows its boundary,
follows the line of another's watery skeleton, its future shape,
from growing pains to disease.

she takes into account altered blood flow, serum, cervix, the
discovery of fingers.

her father throws her in the pool. she floats.

a meander of hips. the onset of menses and she knows only the
dog will treat her differently.

she turns her hands to my hands, turns the soil in her own
garden, smells like rainwater, pushes out weeds, placenta, poetry.
I still have one milk-tooth when I die, and my mother too, and
my daughter thinks hard about our gums and softly about her
own baby tooth.

she needs a rest, overproduces bone substance in a line traveling
all the way back to her grandfather and back again through me to
her. she wants me to want her to be like me, and I do, wants to
have the hands I have had, the slow curve of fingertip to palm.
she throws her claws into the air as if they were not of her
making. it's a cyclic code that's not understood but written.
while he's alive her husband signs her name.

GABRIELLE CALVOCORESSI

Graves We Filled before the Fire

Some lose children in lonelier ways:
tetanus, hard falls, stubborn fevers

that soak the bedclothes five nights running.
Our two boys went out to skate, broke

through the ice like battleships, came back
to us in canvas bags: curled

fossils held fast in ancient stone,
four hands reaching. Then two

sad beds wide enough for planting
wheat or summer-squash but filled

with boys, a barren crop. Our lives
stripped clean as oxen bones.

WENDY COULTER

Winnowing

A woman struggles to draw circles
freehand, her fist wrinkling around the pencil,

grinding its lead into white sheets of paper
on the dining room table; her eyes squint

toward the burning air, the rye toast
she's been charring to smell her father's love

of smoke. It is quiet, late, and he,
of course, is one of many just dead –

shapes are pushing down through the linen,
etching permanence into the mahogany.

The moisture of an old orange
rests in its dense rind loosely wrapping

dry sweetness; she eats absently
and then, with great care, the woman lodges

a single seed beneath her tongue
as if she could warm it to life, to a tree

that flowers whitely every spring
then lets its blossoms go, or as if she could melt

the seed away, turn time backwards:
see the table etchings become whorled grain,

the table turn back to a broken red tree,
see the cracked walls mend, the roof tiles fly,

one by one, into stacks on the ground,
toast spinning back to staffs of wheat,

the universe collapsing around her, simplified
into the infinite density of a point

that holds the memory of everything
and has nothing yet to grieve.

Radio, Radio

In the middle of every field,
obscured from the side by grass
or cornhusks is a clearing where
she works burying swans alive
into the black earth. She only
buries their bodies; their wings.
She packs the dirt tight around
their noodle necks & they shake
like long eyelashes in a hurricane.
She makes me feed them by hand
twice a day for one full year: grain,
bits of chopped fish. Then she
takes me to the tin toolshed.
Again she shows me the world
inside her silver transistor radio.
She hands me the scythe.

Self-Portrait as Lincoln's Assassin

Gentle is the decision, citizen. In pale
dawn of April I closed
my mouth
around it like gunmetal.

I blame April's kindling, April's
lust, April's ashes. I blame
the curtain
of her filthy night.

I'd planned it grander, but gentlemen,
gentlemen: I pulled back April's eyelid, saw
the twitching
clock-face of her eye.

That giant mute, his bones like
railroad ties, his drooping brow,
all guilelessness.
Everything in the theater was gold.

I was mad calm, lurking behind his
stiff-backed rocker – I paused in
the glare –
Oh palsied colossus, I'd no idea

there was so little of him, that he'd wear
such a bad old suit – my tiny pistol parted
her lips,
glittering, as if to kiss his temple

and he froze, my ladies, he knew.
His beautiful dull eyes fixed ahead, I

emptied myself
into the pink sweetmeat of his brain.

There is no manger for what I did. I was told
we could still win and I didn't
quite believe. It was Good Friday and April turned on her heel,
pitiless.

ELLEN VINZ

Dalton, Wisconsin, Late January

Today I'm sorting pennies. My grandparents' coin collection,
saved in a shoebox for years. Liberty dime. Buffalo
nickel. Another America: long grasses bend in the breeze,
a lost ocean of wheat. Here and now: slush and small backyard.
The clocks tick and my grandmother sifts insurance claims
at the kitchen table. After fifty-three years, she is no longer
married. Funeral yesterday. I don't know
what to say so I catalogue pennies by year. Heads or tails.
Thought I found an Indianhead, but it's an ordinary
wheat. Neighbors bring ham sandwiches, funeral food.
New widows don't cook; she sorts through old
hunting licenses and government bonds. Flotsam,
duck stamps, wedding ring. I tell her to keep the pennies;
they're not worth much. Just to have around. My hands
smell of ham and warm metal, of heartland. Minted in Denver.
1943, when the home front changed copper pennies to steel. War
wedding. My grandfather, barrel-chested in a borrowed suit.
Corn to plant, but first the wedding photo. He will change
into overalls right after, go out to feed the hogs and check the rain
gauge. His crooked smile will be passed down to his eldest son's
eldest daughter in thirty-six years. My grandmother
stares into the lens, seeing something else. Ordinary wheat. A
vacancy. Four sons.

JERRY WILLIAMS

A Fine Powder

He had a little box that looked like a dark brown treasure chest
with an iron gargoyle for a lock.

He had a grainy whetstone that he kept
in an aqua blue pouch with Chinese lettering.

I have no idea who he was; he died and I'm getting paid
to tear the dry-wall out of his house with a claw hammer.

That box has a red velvet lining; it's got keys in it, matches,
the tassel from a graduation cap.

There's no money, not that I would take it,
but there's a spent shotgun shell
and a pink guitar pick with teeth marks all over it.

I can't promise that I won't demolish this house.
Delicateness makes me lonely and loneliness makes me vicious.
I keep a sledgehammer in the truck.

But undoubtedly a pattern exists here.
A dead man lies in state, his face clean-shaven, expressionless.
The telephone rings and a forged voice says,
Do you still have my knife?

Undoubtedly, a pattern.
Maybe it's better to disavow the small things.
The opposite of a miracle hovers above this spare estate,
looking for a tongue, a teller.

KIRK LEE DAVIS

In the Greenroom: The Rhyming Couple

What is this green for if not renewal? – Donald Justice

The family down from them got no sleep that night.
                                        – Havit L. Fisher

A shirt made of coins, a hat of bees,
an absence of elbow-joints –
and they're dancing!

They wear their shoes out every night.
They dance a furious stationary.
They dance the six-foot leapback.

The man dances into a dry spell.
The woman's hands are a pink bowl.
The man drinks what he needs.

They dance themselves Christian,
then they dance themselves back again.

They dance so hard the trees fall down inside them.
They dance so loud nobody can hear.

The coins rain into the floor which is the soil.
They dance them down like they were planting.

RACHEL DEWOSKIN

Love Poem from South China, 1999

The tropical infection traced
a map up my finger and standing
outside the Kunming Red
Cross Hospital, we watched this white

rabbit eat Christmas poinsettia
before we found the Doctor named Wen.
Registration for the operation cost 3 kuai 5
equivalent to twenty-seven cents. Dr.

Wen pointed two fresh, ready fingers
at his table and repeated (in English)
operation. After the lecture on pus
and abscess, you expressed nonchalance

at the sight of his knife, (he unwrapped
it, you said, optimistic) and I
whispered translations into the shirt
where I buried my face at your waist.

When Dr. Wen sliced the finger like tropical
fruit the leather taste spread
to the back of my mouth. *Operation,*
your belt, Chinese vocab abscess

operation, white rabbit, red plant. The day
went on outside, and when I
noticed it again hours later, I had stopped
screaming, The bandages were just

gauzy hotel curtains, angels
in fluttering light. When I rolled
from the shadows of hospital shock,

you introduced me to
my finger. Gored and masked
criminal bandit! Escaped from the red
cross, you said: Finger X. Read
a passage from *Our Man*

In Havana. Yes, China, Havana
nary a trauma; we double wrapped the
digit's disguise with a plastic shower
cap and swam off the coast

of Hainan. But just to be safe, you carried
me through the water
with my hand raised like a torch
above the waves.

RACHEL GALVIN

Letter Spoken in Wind

Today we walked the inlet Nybøl Nor
    remembering how to tread on frozen snow.
        Ate cold sloeberries

that tasted of wind – a white pucker –
    spat their sour pits in snow. Along
        the horizon, a line of windmills dissolved

into a white field. Your voice
    on the phone, *a gesund auf dein keppele*
        you blessed my head. Six months now

since I've seen you. There are
    traces of you here, your curls still dark
        and long, your woven dove,

the room you stayed in: send your syllables,
    I am swimming below the tide-
        mark. Words shed overcoats, come

to me undressed, slender-limbed, they have no
    letters yet. It is the festival
        of lights, I have no

candles. I light one for each night,
    pray on a row
        of nine lighthouses.

Digging Potatoes, Sebago, Maine

Summer squash and snap-beans gushed
all August, tomatoes in a steady splutter

through September. But by October's
last straggling days, almost everything

in the garden was stripped, picked,
decayed. A few dawdlers:

some forgotten carrots, ornate
with worm-trail tracery, parsley parched

a patchy faded beige. The dead leaves
of potato plants, defeated and panting,

their shriveled dingy tongues
crumbling into the mud.

> You have to guess where.
> The leaves migrate to trick you. Pretend
> you're sure, thrust the trowel straight in,
> hear the steel strike stone, hear the song
> of their collision – this land is littered
> with granite. Your blade emerges
> with a mob of them, tawny freckled knobs,
> an earthworm curling over one like a tentacle.

I always want to clean them with my tongue,
to taste in this dark mud, in its sparkled scatter

of mica and stone chips, its soft genealogy
of birch bark and fiddleheads, something

that means *place,* that says *here,*
with all its crags and sticky pines,

its silent stubborn brambles. This
is my wine tasting. It's there,

in the potatoes: a sharp slice with a different blade
imparts a little milky blood, and I can almost

smell it. Ferns furling. Barns rotting.
Even after baking, I can almost taste the grit.

MOLLY LUBY

On Jimmy's Front Porch, His Momma Does My Hair

In plaits not braids, and whistles
out complaints through the comb,
held like a pirate's knife in her teeth,
each time my hair limps and simpers
its way free of her hands.
She breathes words, heavier than air,
dusty words, like Georgia clay before rain,
which she, in fact, eats from a bucket
beside the chair, an old metal kitchen thing
dragged out each morning and in each night.
She says lord or honey or girl before everything.
"Lord Jimmy, get your black butt here where I can see,"
or "Lord honey, it's *damn* cold," and "Honey girl, sit still."

"Honey babe, how's your momma?"

I bet if I talked my words would look like taffy
left too long in the sun, so soft and angry
they'd get stuck in your teeth.
My mother's words are sunshine and glass,
see-through words that look different
from the corner of your eye and grow
warmer the longer you sit under them.
They are kind as questions,
smart as beetles' antennae.

I've got no one to talk to anyway, is what I think
when Jimmy teaches me to run like they do in Kenya.
In Kenya, he shows me, you put your hands like this.
Flat as steel knives, they slice up space
and he just steps on through – gone,
clean and fast as a curtain falling over the sun.

What I Wish

Mr. Sato slips into conversation with me
the way a petal drops from a cherry tree.
Mt. Yoshino has a fat waist girdled with three thousand cherry trees
    according to him.
Am I just in feeling flattered?
It's a rare feeling even in spring,
and his fingers are moving like translucent white baits.
I like repeating his name *Sato,*
drunk on its unoriginal resonance;
I even like his watercolor face
on the verge of merging with the rest of the scenery.

Mr. Sato shows me how to prepare arrowroot jelly.
There are more Satos than all the blossoms put together
    at Mt. Yoshino each spring,
but he is the Sato who makes arrowroot jelly.
I am not learning, not really –
I am busy thinking
I won't see New York again, even in a dream,
and how much sweeter my disposition will be once I become
    Mrs. Sato,
how much more civil, my world. For the final touch now,
Mr. Sato's hand lets float salted petals on top of his jelly
in the manner nondescript and slightly feminine.

*

It hurts to think
we are not having tea for real.
Are we thirsty? Who has invited whom?

In the room next to ours,
girls in white uniform walk in procession
on equinoctial amaryllises back and forth,

back and forth,
Because the character for butterfly in their language
is so beautiful, it is unbearable.

Suddenly, I seize you by the wrist:
as if having been bruised just now,
butterflies surface in blue-black ink.

"Sunflower tea warms you
even on a rainy day," you tell me,
but there is no such tea, and there is no rain
starting either from above or below us.

JILL OSIER

A Bringing Back

A certain kind of house attracts a bluebird.
I saw a special once on how a young girl hoped to build
enough birdhouses in her town to bring them back.

My grandfather knew birds. I think he may have loved them – more
   than drinking
or working wood, since in the end these got too hard. Year after year
he knew they'd return despite his orneriness. He could watch them from
his shop or the kitchen, where finally, in one of his chairs,
he mostly cursed and wheezed as he rocked.

I'm not sure where the old one came from,
hanging from the maple in my folks' yard. Last year
the wire that held it broke, lay poking up
out of the leaves, and the damn thing still hung somehow.

Early spring and cloudy, my brothers and I drive gravel roads.
We pass old farmhouses, weedy creeks, pastures fighting through fence
   line
They sit in front, recalling where as kids they'd gotten drunk and stuck
in field mud. I sit in back and imagine the young girl in her raincoat,
nailing her rough, homemade houses up to fence posts. I might see flecks
of color in the ditch, and they might be the earth deciding to forgive.

In my family, this has always been the invitation home: wood
started a long time ago, and there's plenty lying around. You strip it,
work it down, and make it good again.

JULIE SOPHIA PAEGLE

Estuary and Divide

Not far from this shore
        there is a cave
                stunned with silver strung through its thresholds:
    milagro upon milagro hanging in the absence
             of ailment and two hundred tons of rock,
    stalagmites spangled with miniature and diminishment,
limbs bent and battered in metal picking up candle light and miracle –

   Tell this limestone
            that miracles always occur in spite
                       of themselves, and divide

the self from faith!
           Tell this row of small silver calves about the eye
of a needle, these dangling feet that they
                  should not need any shining
idols, any flame   this column will grow around the curving grey arms –
     when the sea rushes the cave again
          the rock will grip many dented metal hearts –

At tidewater
           reeds rise
       from riverbottom to this: self-
          parting at the surface where insects skid and jump valences:
substance split to ions
      electric sleights of shadow ripple down the waters, shadow and all
muted by groundfog, or mist, or troposphere dropped and scattered –

                    around these reeds,
                              where they wear their shadows,
                                                  some silver –
hand, lung, two horses –

                    That they float on salt
                              in the shadow of a reed *is*
faith and not its caving, not its insistence, but the quiet litter of its
    presence,
          that they are here where river bottoms out to the sea,
where the waters mix salt with crushed mountain, pounding out the
    quartz – *this is*
for everything that parts in moving, reed, tuft, river –
                    that these small made pieces made their way here,
                              to this place in the pull of the moon, dull and among
waterbeetle and mist –

from *The Thirteen Books*
(BEING A SECTION OF *The Pillow Book*)

light was sheltered from them. their ink, bodies caught in the rain. *is this where the body begins,* they asked. *where the ink binds skin & language.*

this is where language begins, they replied. their lips caught the words in silence. *this is where the ink binds the body & its words.* their stories were those of writing, of the book turned flesh when the lover falls silent.

they turned them into pillows, into the sheets we wrap our words in. their skin bound our myths, our secrets, as the book itself is bound in our bodies.

where does the book end, they asked.

it ends with our silence, they replied. *when the final page becomes the sepulcher from which we read, are read, & continue to write. though in death our words escape the silence that bound them in life. the book writes as we are written, as the words upon your body become the book upon which we sleep.*
*

the pressure of a brush upon the skin. needle, sheets of bamboo. the skin is punctured, ink inserted within. these motions are repeated, until the text begins to appear.

these methods are ancestral, they said, *the texts themselves arise from the muscle.*
*

they came from within the skin, their ink bled itself into their words.

she imagined her body as being given to sound. to the image of a page, a script undecipherable.

her notebook was her body, the analogy of time, or the becoming of time, it appeared as if speech was the language of the mute. *they didn't speak,* she wrote, *until the hours of their book vanished* into their silence.

the images appeared in sequences, brief flashes of both word & world, spirits of the vanished.
*

you had asked me to write of the sun. the unwritable book, the book of beginnings & of births.

they existed in legends, in the randomness of story.

I had thought distance as one does the self as the imagination turned inward.
*

time itself is calligraphic, he said.

time itself is the doubling of the page.
*

they titled the book, the book of the lover, *in which the text discovers its twin.*
*

1 could imagine nothing but letters, she wrote.

the book burns itself into our births.

Years of Age

ball of yarn, lonely frigate;
each minute a day, each day a month,
you get the picture, you do the math;
the imagination like the clouds a fist on the horizon,
invented from the inside like a tree,
invented from the outside like "a tree"
is a paper boat adrift on an arbitrary system
of waves; meaning I'm open but not too open,
etc.; the novel beginning "He,
stranded across the heathery hills dappled
with rain" & "awaiting orders via the luminous chateau
where heels count casualties across the marble floor";
facial hair, its removal photographed in stages,
as in: "The Seduction of Marie,"
as in the poem that begins: My love is
like an ice cream truck / it rings its bell for you;
burns up on re-entry; "The Architecture of Fear,"
the agriculture of Peru; how the heart
resembles mostly a fist-knot of arteries,
how the heart is a fist, a harbor,
a bricolage; last seen toiling as an extra on the set
of "The Fugitive Kind" circa 1950, the sun aswelter,
the humidity a bitch, just to catch a glimpse
of angelic Joanne Woodward;
O asomatic years of age,
nothing can touch you because there is
no "outside," an amazing trick, you predict yourself,
your wings flap a little & a dust storm kicks up
in the attic of l'histoire de la folie; or not, I'm drunk
drinking gin from a mason jar,
putting the strophe back in catastrophe,
see: "black box," "black boot," "ich, du"; see:
dusk's blushing decolletage; the sentence beginning

"if one replaced hymen w/ marriage or crime";
the night beginning with women walking
outside the window; the "walkers" & the "distance walked";
O years of age, ball of wax,
the ice melts, the nights drops trou;
sometimes it's enough

KRISTINE SOMERVILLE

The Turbulence of Liquids

My cat lounges in ripples of light the panels of glass cast on the floor. He has been out all night, his eyes lit red by an on-coming car, before he shoots across the street, a flash of white like a child's ghost or a bit of quick moving fog. Beneath the widow's bird feeder he waits, and, in the morning, as the sun rises over the treetops and the night colors fade from purple to pink, I find a starling on my doorstep, goat-eyes closed, head lightly resting on its small, black breast. Another time, I found a pigeon, eyes shadowed dramatically like a movie star's, the beak, outlined like lips. Both birds were seemingly untouched except for the tail feathers scattered. My cat yawns. The skeletal roof of his mouth is visible from where I sit on the couch, reading about Oppenheimer's apprentice, a man who experimented with twenty-six hour days. Often, he woke to the setting sun. The red glow of his cigarette floated in the dark as he walked the streets thinking about the turbulence of liquids. Later, when he confined himself to parking lots, the morning revealed his tracks, imagined bands of fluids turning clockwise, counter clockwise, as if the snow-covered ground was the surface of Jupiter and he, a satellite, capturing the image for the first time.

JENNIFER J. UNDERSTAHL

The Ghost Town I Live in Has Signs
That Say: Keep Out

The one gas-station attendant
shines his pump. I love no one

right now. It's that easy
to get by here.

Night skies
are very dangerous –
too close.

It's not nice to lock your door.

When the streets flood,
I walk barefoot. The water

moccasins drip from trees.
No one weighs me down –

                    my leisurely arms.

Prairie dogs alert one another
when I approach their yellow fields,

balding grass. A livestock train takes
its time – I can hear

metal sections trying to close
their gaps. Click, click, click . . .

If I stay away from idle conversations,
I will not grow old.

MILES WAGGENER

Antonio Machado and the Trees

Baeza, 1915

The poet is eavesdropping on the sycamores
at dusk. They talk with the copper light, the wind
they trap with long, knotted fingers –
their shapes racing against the chipped walls
of the village where he has banished himself at forty
to live with his mother, now that his child bride
has been two years in the grave. In the light
and chatter of the trees, the poet is resolved
to die teaching children French,
to live out what's left, years shipwrecked in a sea
of smoldering olive groves, the small pleasures
of regular verbs and nightfall in rural Spain.
He has only to read the gossip of the trees,
their talk of the lost bride. *Leanor,* they say how fragile
she was when they married, and how consumption
riddled her away from him. The sycamores know
there was so little left of her that he secretly wanted
to carry her coffin like a guitar case
against his chest, with neither company nor ceremony,
all the way to the grave. As the day fades, the trees
mutter in their ranks before the last light leaves them.
The conversation is over. The poet, ashamed,
and exposed on his hill, shivers
among the silent arches, the dark plaza,
where lions bite down on the brass rings of the doors.

ANNA ZIEGLER

Sunlight in a Cafeteria, Edward Hopper, 1958: Sketches

First he worked with people, then with light
in small pencil drawings – studies in perspective.
Then the chair, the leafy plant, the revolving
door (twice – inside and out), the tables (beside them,
directions detailing the distance from one to the other),
the cafeteria from the outside – plain, gray –
which, ultimately, we do not see. Others:
her arms resting on air, a bracelet stuck halfway
between wrist and elbow, his hand, two sets of legs,
one thick, one thin, both hers.

*

These were penciled lightly, but light is heavy.
In 1958 – breath on the pane, waiting-time – Hopper made
a sail of light, this woman and man his crew.
Beneath the sail, the sea is still, frozen in time: 1958.
It is winter, and this a small part of winter.
Will they speak? In the drawings, earlier,
they are married, in love, their hands touch bashful
beneath all that light, like a bower. But, with time,
the echoes fade, and the walls of the cafeteria
curve inwards until talk is crowded out.
He eyes the leafy plant, she watches her hands,
hitting against each other on the table. Nothing else happens;
they have passed each other by. But the sea is still frozen here,
the sail upright, mast draping over them,
like everything that is yet to come.

*

Hopper's words are scrawled in pencil on these sketches.
Some are directions – silver table-leg, pale yellow table-top,
brass clock, gray-blue building. I imagine other words:
tired eyes, dry-cleaned blouse, torn stocking. Anxious hands,
jumpy legs (bouncing beneath the pale yellow), hunger.
The sketches are arranged in three frames. The first holds three,
the next, four, and the last, seven. I touch the frames,
though I am not supposed to. They get bigger, quickly,
as we do. I remember my grandfather saying to me, a kid,
"the only thing faster than an aero-plane is how fast
you grow." He loved the word "aero-plane." I like
the idea of Living Art. I think these sketches grow like life.

*

Even when in love, they are not in control, but
Hopper is. He has made her eyes worried
with a pencil, filled his cup with brown coffee.
He has emphasized the light, because he knows what is constant
and what is not. Their heads are cut from light,
triangular above, like a sail. One must wonder
where this boat has been, where it will go.
As boats do, it will not stay. Next perhaps to a child-filled
playground in early autumn, a spot for coasting
between clouds like a kite. Or, mellow, drift
across city streets in 1978, twenty years later,
after all is said and done. But, first he will use it again,
in motel rooms, gas stations, on Cape Cod. Finally, in an Empty
Room, in 1963, no longer poised. Mark Strand called it
"Hopper's last great painting, a vision of the world
without us," for it is what we are not: only light,
expanding from outside to inside, in two quick
snatches of rhythm, beating.

MEG ARENBERG

From a Small Window

Afternoon now, the heat eases around me,
splays a ragged oval across my forearm.

Yesterday I left morning, crisp cut
in Michigan, skimmed lake water

with my toes. There,
it was the raw smell

of autumn. It was piles of sand.
I walked my mind all over.

Now, rising, I watch the river
widen, unlabeled, below.

Watch what it is. Through the clouds,
a silver sleeve unwrapping.

What, spidery, shimmering,
if not eternity? Watervein

whose breath I take up, even here,
the stretch of space between us.

I'm nowhere. Left to watch
the before and after.

The tiny white roofs,
spreading from the fold of silver.

Like ash, like circumstance.

TERRI K. BORCHERS

Scar and Story

A yellow air mattress fading into sea froth,
late autumn light on the shore,
that plot of beach some many-paned portal

on the universe – when my friend's Pop hurried
across the sand, all she and her little sis

could do was point at the plastic rocking
up and down on the blue that stretched
to all those places hidden by an edge.

Where was her cousin Jess? The two knew nothing
of undertows, how a body

could disappear for months.
The funeral seemed all candles,
her aunt Pat's gray face, a parade of iris,

empty box and songs. The chapel
in so many colors her Mom wanted

to recall, somebody hurried my friend
back to car for a camera, she tripped
in the gravel. Large as a nickel

in the middle of her right kneecap, the scar
an open eye that still stares

whenever she folds herself bare-legged
into a chair, tries to loll to calm
in a tub. Her Dr. B said she

should've had stitches, but no one
could be bothered. Her cousin drowned,

or that's what she tells me: how a family
invents a past to comfort; she's taught herself
to please, assuage, through memory –

another gift to tie back up once untied –
since no one said it, suicide, she swears,

when her Aunty left her five years later.
At eleven she had to know better,
she tries to explain; learned early

we can choose – even to go – and language,
how well we're taught in wordless times,

is the only honest blessing, gift, good-bye.
That giant we, and how her Mom
wouldn't say why she wouldn't attend

the service; couldn't see why her Pop
made her go, pulled the yellow mattress

from the glass-doored cupboard in his den.
Only six when he scrubbed out the hole
in her knee with Neosporin, patched it tenderly

with gauze and cloth tape's stubby flannel fingers –
more sure than any tale she's yet to patch together –

called her years later at camp when Aunty died.
His voice calm as a tool chest: never mention
a body's makeshift moorings, family code.

Perhaps that's how he's held on, she tries
some more to persuade me, a lighthouse beacon

easing a prow round a pier past dusk,
still seems to move like a master
through consanguinity's red embrace

with time. Her cousin, I don't know,
maybe he found peace – that fickle

but stubborn peace of the surf
fantasy abuses helplessly,
scar and story never close or open.

JENNIFER CHANG

The Skin's Broken Aria

I cross the street
and my skin falls off. Who walks
to an abandoned lake? Who
abandons lakes? I ask questions
to evade personal statements. When you are
skinless, you cannot bear to be
more vulnerable. With skin, I
would say *I am in love with*
Love as in that old-time song
crooners like to croon. With skin,
I would wear elbow-length opera gloves
of pearly satin. Protect my skin.
Hide it. There is no skin
like my skin. How I miss it –
I miss it as I would a knitted bonnet, a
pewter teaspoon to stir sugar into hot water.
My great passion was my skin. The lover
I loved. They don't
sell skin at Wal-Mart. And really, how
could I, humanely, buy it? Would you ever
give me your skin? This is a terrible world
we live in. There are mistakes and
batteries littering a junk drawer,
where Mother would hide my house keys and Father
would store his eyeballs. Do you know
Puccini? Do you spill silk
at the gorgeous onslaught of love, of Pinkerton's
lurking return? Butterfly had no skin either
but you could not tell from the outer left
balcony. As I lay in a bed
of my dead skin, I dream of Butterfly
and what she could have done instead:
run away to this little room

to lose her aching voice, to listen
to the hourly ringing of bells
that is really the souring birdsong
of a child, skinned and
laughing, a child that will never be hers.

The Farrier's Daughter

As a Child, I would awake to the staccato
of restless horses, black and sweet-limbed,
against the unkempt acres.

I thought they would know my scent. After all,
I was my father's daughter –
well versed in the ritual of cattail and starling.

Velvet noses bumped my offered palm,
then turned away into the crease of a late hilltop sun.
They punished my father for his devotion:

grew lame, burred their slick coats,
opened themselves to spill gelled stillborns
onto the loose hay. I saw grief

soak his hands like an anointing. And then, the moon
shattered in their smooth, black eyes
glanced off the metal of upturned hooves

the night Topaz Ore knelt and did not stand again.
That steel caress on an aged temple
was enough to indict us all,

even the wavering pines. I cast only
the slightest shadow
against the gray crooked fence, knowing

that they needed someone to blame
as I did
for a gunshot amid the honeysuckle,

for crickets, lost to me in this city,
for callused hands that could not stop,
did not try to stop my own silver flight.

YOSEFA RAZ

I charge you, O daughters of Jerusalem

Who do I sing to?
– train tracks parting
apartment buildings like a seam
to allow in the sky;
the uneven pavement
bursting with weeds.

Though I sing to the daughters of Jerusalem
I also sing to the new daughters of Davis,
and the disheveled daughters of Sacramento;
to my infant sister Elianna, who I have never seen,
whose pictures arrive by airmail in pale yellow envelopes,
to Kalliope, waving her hands in the air at Baker's Square;
to daughters protected by their mothers
from their fathers,
with and without good reason.

Daughters of Jerusalem,
my lover is not waiting at the end of the pool
when I finish the lap breathlessly,
he is not selling dried apricots at the farmer's market,
he is not walking his dog on the empty streets.
He is the sound of the bathwater,
which is the sound of a waterfall,
which is the sound of mercy.

If you see my lover,
Daughters of Jerusalem,
emerging from the early-morning fog,
steam rising from the Civic Center Pool –
ask him, how to become interested in your own courage.

Tell my water lover
to swallow his words

until he is soft enough to lean on.
Tell my lover that the window is open,
and the bed is empty.

Daughters of Jerusalem,
you've gone far from Jerusalem
to escape re-elections,
political talk-shows that turn into screaming matches,
your mothers.

Now you're turning up in the green belt,
or in the dog park near the cemetery;
the hems of your white dresses are dotted with organic mud.
You hide between trees of black walnut.

Do not be lonely.
Decorate your braids with orange poppies
that grow on the ramps beside the overpass,
for even your name is beautiful.

JILL TREMBLAY

Corn Carnival

They praised corn for one weekend
In August, at the edge
Of a season, when fingers
Tasted of roasted husks
& left salt grains in prints.
Tongues, in this month, started
To drag – papillae choked
By a membrane of butter.
They talked from their throats
With voices like albumen
Bleeding through eggshell cracks.
Bodies lined up at the tent
To celebrate Minnesota farms
Over paper plates loaded with cobs
& bent like fiberglass rods
Under the weight of muskellunge.
They said yellow was the burn
Of the sky on their necks,
& the smell of a mother's hands
Unbraiding silk between kernels.

Literal

The geese are bolted
to the green. They've reached
consensus, common ground

on winter grass. To make feast of survival
never occurs to them – they'd make
survival of a feast. They're literal,

bird for bird. The sky is empty
of each one. We also grace
what we can graze

but have so much in mind.
Forgetting is a feat.
Shut out by memory, that dollhouse

fully furnished in a scale
we can't inhabit, we're still entranced.
Love too plays tricks. In trains

stopped side by side, motion in one
misleads the other. So much
descends with purpose.

The flight we know, but not
to hunger accurately:
the sparrow's eye the exact

size of a seed, the geese
offering the grass no tenderness
it does not offer back.

JAMES ARTHUR

A Sequence For Birds

Let's begin at the window, with my neighbour
counting birds with her daughter

who cannot walk and will never learn speech.
Numbers for pigeons: *one.* In the sky's coal smudges

the bird becomes lost. The girl's eyes
are still polished nothings. If you cannot understand me,

track me sentimentally: read the poem,
I will love you, it will be uncomplicated.

Imagine yourself training children to be birds –
nuzzle, kiss, release, fly!

Sequences, we trust, lead us somewhere
while birds disappear over the cat's cradle of wires.

RACHEL BECK

Obedience: There Are Two Kinds

We can obey the force of gravity or we can obey the relationship of things.
— Simone Weill

Oh, wag, Sirius says, and good mornings the book out of my hands. We are out
for a walk, bristleback branch-lively, even before I have washed my eyes,
everything I see through a forecast of clouds, lent by a walk in the park.

He stops to be territorial and shoots himself on the foot. South toward the dam,
from this distance the water looks immobile, the color of cars, close attention is
    not enough,
Claudia says, so late in our history, be absolutely quiet in hopes of lengthening.

Even at the hour when the joggers are thickest, we are separated
by the shapes of our leads. I love, my love, through a pane of glass, your eyes
    have changed
color, the streaks and shine are the death of us. Some fears are untouched by
    exaggeration.

Let's cross the street, monstrosity, stranger-than-fiction is coming for us,
from this distance his mouth in floral profusion, red, teetery in the region not
    for gossip.
Under our feet is zoned warmer.

Legion of angels, poster children,
I hope not all ardor is theatrical, least of all mine for the sandwich shop, cashew
    butter
dotted thick with raisins. I have said I need, I need, when I do not need, days on
    loan.

In the steeple someone is ringing the changes, bells unweighted
by a sense of return. Whoever used the eyes of god going home from you
gave them for ornaments. Let me have it then, a war on montage:

in mud, the smell of wet oak leaves overrides the smell of dry oak leaves.

JOHN ERHARDT

Penis

Let's face it: everyone knows a monologue when they see one.

Hand over the children, you said.
Each morning, the silent lobbyist goes to work.
I provide a splendid hour of gossip.

I am a proud elected official with two idiot secretaries.
A 24-Hour gambling helpline.
Once the world stops suspecting me, I reconfess.
I have mastered the genre of addendums.

I am granted thousands of pardons each month.

MARGARET FUNKHOUSER

Crown

The paramount, the high water
mark. Cornices and crow's nests, a ruling
in the belfry. With finials
and fontanelles, I croon a meridian

hymn to the metonym: mantle
of ermine, diadem of influence.

Under this sway, I am viceroy.
The monarch's potentate of counterpoise.
Prescient that in the precious there
is also something awful. Garniture

vases, resigned to a museum
basement. The finest letters pressed inside
a book's decrepit bind. Candied
violets, an ocean's luxury line,

jeweled hatpins and delicate blue
stockings. The beautiful awaits to be

forgotten by that which is not.
Dear Sovereign, I am thrown by many things –
Ardent garters and dexterous
emblems. Heraldic crests of cormorants.

Aunt Ida's Box

Aunt Ida's box got a ticket for the EI, rose petals
dropped to dust, and teeth. Cuban cigars, I can
still smell them. Mama curls her lip. "I always
said that woman was perverse. Shoulda had her
own to get ridda her things."

*

A surgeon – still available – extracted her
ivory   She left him in St. Louis,
kept the teeth – the roots like legs
kicking high as Ziefgield girls –
She kept them dancing
in her box

*

Husband number four stoops toward the
others whispering like church, *In her day* –
Mama snorts. "How it really was, she caught
men like trains. Rode 'em. Used 'em up. Got
off at the next stop."

Ida's rose bush gray.

Uterus donated to science.

*

In her day, my god!
her twat was tight

Three story walk-up
The girls plugged in irons, curlers,

every Friday night the power blew
From the ice box
they took ceramic fuses
the size of buttermilk biscuits,
climbed ladders, laughing,
swapped hot ones out with oven mitts
The men
passed them, came

flickering toward
the bloom of Ida's rooftop Pall Mall,
stained their 4 a.m. lips, fingers

Don't imagine I didn't do it
Fuck like mad –

bear witness

*

Mama throws the box in the
Goodwill bag. "Ain't nothing
here you can use."

Ida's crowns press stars in my palm.

Mama,
In her day –

ANN HUNKINS

Watching the Mahabharata

Every week we watch the Mahabharata on tv
   upstairs in the landlord's apartment.
We balance on round little stools.
   You are irritated that I don't understand Hindi
the way every Nepali speaker does.

   The streets are silent when the Mahabharata is showing;
shops roll down their shutters, the campus is deserted.
   You watch intently: one of the King's sons plucks a foam
column from the wall of the palace,
   raises it over his head and shouts something
to a crowd of warriors who frown under mascara and rouge.
   "What did he say?" I ask but you don't react.
The screen cuts to a woman in a sky blue,
   gold-trimmed sari holding up a fresh white boy's shirt
just produced by her scrubbing with
   a new cleaning powder.

You listen to the old landlord, who complains that the communists
   are wrecking the new democracy,
while his wife sits hiked up on the cushions,
   popping pink candies into her mouth and breathing
heavily, staring at the screen.
   She calls to her niece to fry us each an egg
and bring tea. You agree the coalition members don't
   get along as well as they did thirty years in prison.

Now there are three bearded men walking in a forest.
   They discover an old man inside a cave, his hair longer than
his body, all matted with twigs and leaves.
   The screen cuts to a young woman wearing golden bracelets,

singing in her shining kitchen, with her full-size refrigerator,
    stove, silver-glistening sink and other appliances.
She's making instant coffee which she brings to her husband
    where he sits at a glass table in the garden.

The landlord remembers the 1934 earthquake, when Kathmandu
buckled like a fish and streets broke like sheets of ice,
    how the clock tower crumbled right where he'd been standing.
The niece brings fried eggs and beaten rice.
    There's a generator grinding outside
to power the tv, lights, and small electric burner for
    frying eggs in pools of mustard oil. It's load-shedding on Thursdays,
and our apartment is dark like the rest of the neighborhood.
    After the show we'll go downstairs and climb under
a ten-pound quilt in a bed sized for a family of five.
    You always want to make love, and I never do.
In the morning you're often gone already.

In the next scene a man appears at the doorway
    of a crumbling stone house, confronts a tiny
old woman with heavy gold earrings,
    spits out three harsh words to her
I don't understand and no one explains.
    My attention wanders. This version is going to take a year,
and we're only in the seventh week.

You eat your egg and rice with your right hand and never look at me.
    We've finally returned to the scene with the King's son,
the foam pillar in the hands of the wax-moustached
    man in long braid and large biceps.
He shouts the same word he shouted at the beginning.
    The crowd draws back, terrified. He makes a stiff bow,
then wades into them with the pillar.
    The power comes back on with a surge, a light bulb over the tv pops.
The niece goes downstairs to shut off the generator.
    The hero knocks down the jeweled warriors like bowling pins
and laughs. He tosses the pillar away and exits
    the ruined palace.

SEAN NEVIN

Losing Solomon

We estimate a man by how much he remembers.
                    – Emerson

Things seem to take on a sudden shimmer
before vanishing, the polished black loafers
he wore yesterday, the reason for climbing
the stairs, even the names of his own children

are swallowed like bright coins into the plush
folds of the mind. Today the toaster gives up
its silver purpose, becomes an old radio blaring
a ball game from the 40s, as Jackie Robinson

squares up to the plate. For now, it is simple, Solomon
is young again, maybe nineteen, alone in a kitchen.
He is staring through the toaster's reflection and hoping
against hope that Robinson will clear the bases

with a ball knocked so far over the stadium wall
it becomes a pigeon winging up into the brilliance.
And perhaps, as one last merciful act of alchemy,
as he sails round third, Robinson will transform
the strange and forgotten face

given back in the radio's luster, into something
familiar, something Solomon could take as his own.

The One About the Wolf

Dead, you don't forget my name, my face.
You never wander off. You don't mistake
another's house for yours. You never sleep.

Dead, your tuck-in's done. You never tell
the one about the girl's red hood. You never
snore yourself awake, forget to leave

the door ajar – I believe the wolf
is just your breathing. Dead, you never cook
your cabbage soup. Or shoo me from your glass

of *hozzem blozzem* – bourbon, water, ice.
You never haunt. Or hear me ring the bell.
I wait, but no one answers. You're a truant.

An awful hostess. Dead, you never give
the one about the wolf disguised as child,
malignant as benign, a happy ending.

It tricked us. Swallowed you alive. Inside,
no muffled cries. It's just as well. The woodsman
can't use his bowie knife to cut you out.

You're dead. But now, you don't forget my name
or call me by my mother's. Dead, you never
speak to me. You never bare your teeth.

KATIE FORD

Breaking Across Us Now

I began to see things in parts again,
segments, a pen drawn against the skin
to show where to cut, lamppost through the stained glass
with its etchings of light against the wall –
it was the middle of the night. It was something we would tell no one:
The hospital roads with standing water, I drove quickly through,
saying, you won't have to stay.
                                        But then I left without you,
you whom I've felt missing all this time –
when I sat in the weeds of the yard, told to pull them
from the root, not to touch the wild trillium, tying knots in the daffodil stalks,
discontented. When I watched the scatters
of firs sway their birds out through my storm windows,
the tree itself now and no more,
I thought I needed belief – walking through the stubbed wheat grass
requesting everything that would undo me – the nearness of Christ,
abandon and devotion – no one has to teach me
my disobediences. No one sees
the shed I see now, its roof bent with snow, all of it
leaning south how it was never built.
The inches overcome it, but
the green wood darkens, oceanic and deep.
                                        He might not wake up,
I thought that night –
                            I remembered the house I boarded in one summer
with a widower, his wife's fabric samples left draped over
the arm of the unfinished chair. I could feel her eyes
in my own when I tried to choose
between them, almost, if the sun of the alcove
hadn't faded them, the dust and his arms worn them.
The sky as stark as the first sheet laid down
after they took her body.
                            But on that night

while I waited, the clouds casketed the stars,
stars with no chambers or hollows, filling themselves
with their own heat how a hive quivers
to fill each crevice with itself,
how I have never been able.

NOTE: *The phrase "Breaking across us now" is from "Easter Morning"*
by A. R. Ammons.

EVA FOSTER

Prizefight

It's night, the crowd's series of pale heads, bored
Or awed, unlocked like the slipped water's O,
The stone thrown in, and on the platform, ringed,
These two shine, one black, one all in red –
Wet heads to shoes laced tight to legs. And sweat.
And when the strikes connect, they seem less blow
Than fall, exhausted, into flesh, one man's
Brow on partner's shoulder till the ref's
Fat hand pulls at this kinder touch – not here,
The sheen of sweat and satin pants alive
With light. Before he stops: the crowd-sound stalls,
Breath-hung, and the fighter, a countless host
Of fires each gleaming, each scale-silver, gasps –
His arm slung round against his other half.

Mosquito

after Herrera

You need evidence of the street
fight? Concrete scabs & a gutter-grate
bruise? Here are nails on the tongue,
a mosaic of glass shards on my lips.
I am midnight banging against house-
fire. The naked woman shaking
with the dense sweat of need.
An ocean of burning diamonds
beneath my roadkill, my hitchhiker
belly fills sweet. I am neon blind & kiss
too black. Dangle stars – let me
sleep hoarse-throated in the desert
with a blanket sewn from spiders.
Let me be delicate & invisible.
Kick my ribs, tug my hair.
Scream *You're Gonna Miss Me
When I'm Gone.* Sing implosion
to this world where nothing is healed.
Slap me, I'll be any kind of sinner.

JONAS LERMAN

Your Grandmother

Her blindness came slow,
like a dusk. A child
in this house, she pulled
at loam, made up names
for nameless smells,
leaned her whole face
into the victrola's horn
just as the RCA dog did.
She could see enough
and touch the rest.
No one told her more.

The blindness grew with her.
By eight, she lived in the dark.
When she told him
finally, her father drove
to town too fast.
She gripped the dashboard,
said *okay, okay, okay.*
No doctor had a name for it.
Each advised patience.
One said vision could come back,
click, like a switch flipped.

The light switches in this house
are black buttons
with pearl in the middle.
You push one in
and the other jumps out.
In the dining room,
her chandelier blinks to life,
surprised. The hallway sconces
flicker, and in the basement

the bare bulb over the furnace
barely glows. You wonder
how she kept these lights up
after her father died, why
she bothered with them.
You duck under the doorframes
and take pictures, holding
your camera chest-level
because that is how tall she was.

In the barn, you check
for bird bodies. She told you
the story of her father
who kept a special pistol
for shooting birds stuck in the barn,

the ammunition fine enough
not to punch holes in the walls.
Nights she heard him
with the birds – a hailstorm
from his barrel, their bodies
twirling into the dirt floor –
and would stand by her window,
one ear to the glass, cupping
her elbows in her palms,
pretending to see them fall.

In the yard, which was an orchard,
you blindfold yourself with a scarf
and stumble to the pear tree,
your camera swinging
around your neck.
You brought only the Polaroid
because you wanted
to capture the house fast,
while you can. You believe
it is genetic, the darkening –
that it skipped a generation,

waited decades for you. Now,
behind her house, you spread
your pictures on the grass
and fan your face with the last one.

It gets late. All the names
for this time sound wrong:
half-light, failing light, dying light,
gloaming, dusk, even *evening.*
You raise your last shot
above your head and tilt it
to the horizon, the final light,
but it isn't finished developing.
The dragonflies arrive around you.
She called them skeeter hawks.
There are no guns small enough,
no ammunition made for them.

The last piece of film
rests on your lap now. Eyes closed,
you pull your arms
through the grass, two scythes.
The dragonflies scatter. You hear them
and look up, and at once
the field becomes a room.
By what light is left, you can see
your last picture come through –
this field you are in, her barn

glowing, her house behind it,
all the windows lit up orange,
each frame burning back the dark.

CATE MARVIN

Lying My Head Off

Here's my head, in a dank corner of the yard.
I lied it off and so off it rolled.
It wasn't unbelieving that caused it
To drop off my neck and lull down a slope.
Perhaps it had a mind of its own, wanted
to leave me for a little while.

Or it was scared and detached itself
from the stalk of my neck as a lizard's tail
will desert its body in fright of being caught.
The fact is, I never lied. The fact is,
I always lied. Before us, we have two mirrors.
At times, they say, one must lie in order

to survive. I drove by the house, passed
it several times, pretending it was not
my own. Its windows were red with curtains
and the honeyed light cast on the porch
did not succeed in luring me back inside.
I never lied. I drove by the house,

suckling the thought of other lovers
like a lozenge. I was pale as a papery birch.
I was pure as a brand new pair of underwear.
It will be a long while before I touch another.
Yet, I always lied, an oil slick on my tongue.
I used to think that I was wrong, could

not tell the truth for what it was. Yet, one
cannot take a lawsuit out on oneself.
I would have sworn in court that I believed
myself and then felt guilty a long time after.

1 hated the house and I hated myself.
The house fattened with books, made me

grow to hate books, when all the while
it was only books that never claimed
to tell the truth. I hated him and I hated
his room, within which his cloud of smoke
heaved. I disappeared up narrow stairs,
slipped quick beneath the covers.

My stomach hurts, I told him, I was tired.
I grew my dreams thick through hot nights:
dear, flickering flowers. They had eyes
which stared, and I found I could not afford
their nurture, could not return their stare,
Meanwhile, liars began their parade

without my asking, strode sidewalks inches
before my doorstep. I watched their hulking
and strange beauty, their songs pregnant
with freedom, and became an other self.
I taught children how to curse.
I bought children gold pints of liquor.

I sold my mind on the street.
1 learned another language. It translates easily.
Here's how: *What I say is not what I mean,*
nor is it ever what I meant to say.
You must not believe me when I say
there's nothing left to love in this world.

SARAH VAP

who knows how long this way

her body's customs
with things

he requires
that she shave
not like a girl

his passing

actually
imagines her own

it's nothing, though

she just climbs out
of the forest
forearms swollen from horseflies,

her eyes swollen –
smears him
on her body, not knowing
how she intends
to live.

So shows
him something –

pollen,
a powerful arm
and vodka
souring his balls.

Nothing left but oldness
she shifts his skin

like a lover
with all this knowledge

of her, he really
had nothing to choose.

JEHANNE DUBROW

Milosz on All Saints' Day

Someone is always kneeling at a grave
or burning votives at the gate. Those cups
of light are the beginnings of ideas.

Then in the church, our voices answer *Pray
for us,* because some ends are certainties,
more certain than chrysanthemums, which fade

a week from now, grow brittle in the cold.
If the Poet pours out his words, scattered
like poppy seeds across the bone-white ground,

the ghosts will masquerade as birds and fly.
Who cares about the dead? They do not hurt.
They cannot feel the dirt wiped from the stone.

When death goes through our house, we open all
the doors, turn mirrors toward the wall to send
the soul away. *Leave us. Leave us alone.*

Places to Put Your Body

1.

In front of the latticework
the gracefully-carved wall
at the back of the men's section:

Wrapped inside your father's tallis
in the smell of silk and aftershave,
leaning your head on his belly,

watching the words his fingers trace
in a leather-bound book:
A congregation of close smells,

where no one is actually reading;
everyone knows the prayer by heart.
You are the only girl.

2.

At night, in the heavy summercamp air.
The boys' bellies are flatter; they
coerce you into damp kisses,

salty, your bodies distant:
you find that you are holding on
to their sharp collars, their belt loops,

just to be sure. Strange kinds
of mornings-after, at prayers,
where you follow along stumblingly.

3.

In Palestine, where the air is hot
and dry, like Los Angeles.
You meet your cousin Akiva

for instant coffee that grates your tongue.
He in his sharp uniform, his crisp green
beret, you wearing your mother's old sandals
and your thinnest sleeveless dress.
You don't touch. Leaving him, passing
checkpoints you can smile

easily through, you smell
the desert, and death
in rotting orchards.

There is the taste of silk
in your mouth; you have bitten
the fabric of men

who have offered to stand guard.
Your skin is darker:
you decide to go home.

The first time you see her is in snow like ermine

The first time you see her is in snow like ermine

The first time   she hears only half-frozen streams

Not your breaking steps   not bare limbs scraping trees

There is no sun   no moon filled gray

Her hair will be tied back and some will fall over her face

You will find her in a thicket of brambles

Where a few blackberries hang dry   where in thorn-tangles

She will be unremarkable and you can't breathe

She will be injured fist

There are leaves and briars frozen under snow

What breaks beneath   your body   she is still alone

You won't call to her though she sighs a red trail to your feet

Each of us will die for a different reason

Invitation

We correspond; wasps in bottles, bottles
In boxes. Or pages like glass leaves, light
Showing veins. Multifoliate prose.
A séance every day we stay apart,
Or telephone schematics in the mail.
Acute awareness flares and fades: the thought
Of us turns filmy, edges curl, and then
Inches away. Disconnects. Stills
Its wings. One day, I will attempt to say
Your name, out loud and facing South, where
I believe you are. Your name a bird of foil
Hatched in my throat, smoothing its pointed feathers
On my soft palette and launching toward your own silence;
My name, bottled up and buzzing.

CYNTHIA ARRIEU-KING

Group Portrait in a Convex Mirror

Now their importance if not their meaning is plain –
They were to nourish a dream which includes them all.
                                        – John Ashbery, "Self-Portrait
                                            in a Convex Mirror"

Like a mosquito eye that never divided into small red honeycomb,
but silver, dipped in something like it, glassy and turned towards everyone.
In the hospital, convex mirror fixed to the ceiling, we see corners meet.
We look into it, like a rearview, and don't bash our stretchers together.

*

I'd met several girls who so reminded me of myself, I was embarrassed
to look at them, their questionable hair, or let one girl know she appeared
in my dream as some version of me, and directed me to lead her, instead
of walking on her own. It was as if I had looked straight into a convex mirror
and instead of seeing only myself, I saw another person,
so similar, the light went through the window and got confused
as to whom should be illuminated in the portrait of solitude. But then,
we thought the better of contrivance, or I did, and twins and quadrads
and everyone started to become lean in the vexing lens, where
like it or not, we were swept together.

*

The faster you push a fat man in a wheelchair, the lighter you both become.
These Lavoisian, Newtonian facts pulled to a taut version of the inner,
small legs slant, push till the weight of solitude, of two beings disperses.
In the convex mirror, there's no direct stare detectable, but room for five, ten,
every soul to chase after her own fact like fish trailing off disparately.
The globe a moment of fluorescent resource, light warning us
To yield to others, seeing them slight, wielding clipboards.
Ashbery, this is insignificance: that is, the colors of the uniforms, navy, or teal,

and the bleak hunch of shoulders tired of pushing other
humans through a warped thoroughfare. In the mirror,
the lights broken into capes, and shifts, white slices
wending masked, and taped. I could never see
a pint of blood hanging from a pole in the distorting mirror.
It takes too long to require our souls are captives only to ourselves.
We would like to stay together. The pause in stride is only recreation.
A myth pains the leg as it slides: that we could all walk
without ever becoming tired.

In the hospital mirror, Old Parmigianino, you painter of solitude,
we receive the brain's just dictates, the decision
between knee and meat, what is now, and what
softly sinks back into a syllabub of dreams and code.
Purse, gait, waste, talk. Us. Seeing a covered gurney in the mirror,
we all know in an instant who will give way, and who move forward.

CHLOE BARNETT

Fairie Lucille Beside Her Sister in Bed

Morrilton, Arkansas, 1925

Just listen out there to those toads,
Ada Mae. It's the best
way I know to fall
asleep, that and thinking
of their saggy eyelids. Remember

how we laughed when we saw them
while we were making mud cakes
underneath the porch?
Up above it was raining. Light
fell between the boards
with the drips but still their eyelids
were heavy as sacks of cottonseed.

Now listen and stop rubbing
your feet on mine. I'm not cold.
Besides, tonight I don't want
to drift off first. To stay awake

I'll stick my knuckles in my ears
and think of the baby snake
I've got back behind the house
under an empty string bean can.
It's black and thin as a ribbon
and at noon I wanted to keep it.

But Ma called me to climb
up on the roof and lay
the peaches out to sun.
So it's out there still in the house
I made with that can and a stone.

And Ada Mae, do you guess
that snakes even have eyelids
to shut? Right now I'll bet
it's slithering around against
the tin listening to its own
long belly whistle in the dirt
like wind. Even if tomorrow

I forget, even if I leave it there
through summer, I'm sure
it'll be grown up and moving
when the boys find it, not a string
of still white bone.

Stones in the Air

The cracking sound above the Freud sisters
is the royal guard shooting black clouds
brimming with hailstones over the Thames.

From the terrace, Anna taps the glowing throat
of a cigarette into her father's skull
he saved from medical school. We are all

emptied, she thinks. Salvador is late
and has been for two years
painting double images – swans,

so unlike hailstones over the water. Ice
stirring the bottom to the surface.
Sophie folds newspaper into origami

birds to float in the melted crook
of her highball. The cut crystal fragments
The Times, tickets to the Ballet Russe,

pictures of trombones, into Braque's collage.
She watches each headline becoming
part of a floating body, blending the ink

in to skin: "The Rookpund Lake
Skeletons" – 600 found by a park ranger –
carbon date back to the 12th century.

How it took seven centuries to find them
broken around a remote lake
in the Himalayas. Their deaths

misdiagnosed – as doctors will do –
landslide, ambush, epidemic. Scooped
    from ice, each skull with the same

fracture. Sudden hailstorm – stones
    as big as cricket balls in the flayed
valley. No cover. Sophie snatches

    the page, turns it into a hat
for Lola barking at cannon shots
    softer than thunder. Patting the dog

near the ashtray, Anna wonders whether
    the animals fled and no one noticed
before the storm, smelling the stones in the air.

BRIAN LEARY

Kindness Becomes Exhausting but We Do It Anyway

They were cashing in on the British invasion & making their own craze.
My parents bought in & did it too. Made lists

of every furnishing in their apartments. Made the give-away piles.

I was a little boy beforehand, but a little girl afterward.
Believe it: I once knew how to run.

God's voice, they said, would come down in bolts. Something big
like every word in one word. We'd know it

when we heard it. One morning my mind snapped shut.

Gerber planned a synthetic & powdered breast milk.
Because there are so many wrong ways to love.

Choose one adjective, my sister said. Already we knew
how to double-dare. Knew some of those bad, bad words.

The *thirteenth* day of life made me nervous. Like wrong way # 4:

don't make promises over breakfast.

Today you will pray so that tomorrow God will be your umbrella.
You, little devil, will be your own rain.

Wrong way # 27: stop lying – tell it like it was: this happened,
then this happened.

I remember crying once into the family water pitcher
to make them all care. But I've made the rest up: my brain was born

on an old German chair lost in the desert. It was lonely.

My head I'm not sure of

but I think someone brought it in from the cold.
If there is a leap in my life, I've reason to come back as a leopard –

you've no more lives so you better be good –

or a clean little hedge. Wrong way # 16: do not admit
your fright. Sometimes late at night, I sing *ob-la-di* in a low tremolo.

Still can't tell if it helps.

MICHAEL PICKARD

Seizure

To my father

Crickets, their flecks of sound softening
the noisome engine; the warnings of the lights
of cars passing, confused; greenhouses rising
from the darkness: where, inside the glinted panes,
an infrastructure of sprig and shoot moistening
is faintly visible. When I awoke, our car
bumped the railing, easy, like a boat against
a dock in choppy water. You don't remember;
the glasses had fallen from your nose. The river
below us slinking into thickets, and in a field
interspersed with hay bales, a juniper.

ELIZABETH RISTOW

How to Play a Musical Instrument

Consider the elephant. He does not
reach or grasp. He extends, acquires

as if the straw were the natural end
of his trunk. Be aware –

your arms have a common goal.
They are tied through your back.

You may feel a slight discomfort.
This is normal, but not

desirable. Seek help immediately.
By elephant, I do not mean

elephantine, nor do I mean grace,
specifically, which is idealized

motion, as well as a prayer.
On the subject of love: this is a process

based on a series of impulses
and reactions. Brahms should not

be used in place of love as
Mozart should not be used in place

of refinement. Dependency is a better
word. Know what is keeping your arm

suspended. Depress the fingers
only as much as needed to make

a sound. Do not think of a marriage,
feather bed, swarm of bees.

ERICA DAWSON

Semantics

Right now I much prefer
Darkie in place of African-
American – the melanin
More obvious. As per
Political correct-
Ness, wait. I'll reconsider Black:
Reflecting little light, a lack
Of predominant hue – effect:
Very dark.

*

          This black, Mom said,
Was born when an up north matriarch
Got hitched back in the day and dark
In Texas. Brillo head
Met roller hair, a lean
And knobby knee wearing a layer
Of darker skin. New jaws curved square
And round. Some aubergine
("Blue black"). Some fair. Some who?
Darkies. Remember? I'm in question.
When a man asked (with suggestion?)

*

"You got Indian in you?"

*

I told him Black and yes.
Characterized by cheerless sullenness,
That lack of light, I incandesce
Pictured in evening dress

And flash. My teeth are white.
The rest: shadow.

*

Perceptions of
Black appear to depend (above)

On the contrast with bright
And colored stimuli.
Black is zero stimulation to
The retina.

*

A vision too
Invisible? I try
To lack for light, eyed closed.
But it's perihelion. Each lamp,
Even the Tiffany, at height
Is pseudo sun exposed.

*

Some days I just see red.

*

Outside, twisting like ivy stems,
My black is brown as periblems
Collecting rains. I want instead

Their pseudonym. Is sheen
Name for their every hue? How true
Lives in perceived. The jigaboo
Moves here with shades of green.

Tribute

This wasn't the first rime or the last,
wasn't the first time we thought of stone or the sparked and flushed light.

The flood was an afterthought of the river and the river that of a greater crime.

This was when names were begotten with a polish of rainwater.

Names are that which we give to what we otherwise forget, which is why I don't
    work for memory

That's one thing and not the other.

I do love your name – how, when I realize the windows are best left open, it
    rolls out like thunder.
The small flood on the sill, too, is an afterthought, but like the river it forgets
    its source to end up in our mouths.

Mouths that keep rivers under the tongue like rumor.

Mouths that sing tribute to storms.

And though it's not the first time, the sill swells in moist air.

And because I don't know the intricacies of a dovetail, it won't be the last, the
    last being a tribute to the labor of clouds in dry season.

This was when we first reclined in advancement.
This was when we skipped stones over tongues of the river.

    This was when.

In labor, a brief river precedes the child.

Through the radio, the siren hums out a rumor of flood.

It's a story I'd rather not tell.

NATHAN GAMACHE

Blessèd are the looters

who place their fists through abandoned glass
and reach around to find the lock. Blessèd

are the looters, every Creole soul, blacks and whites
alike, though one reads that he is stealing, while

the other is said to be stealing back his life.
Blessèd are those who will not wait to be saved.

Blessèd are those who rummage to find vehicles,
then back up stolen goods into the thirsty crowds,

who let anyone who is thirsty, drink; let whoever
is hungry, eat. Let whoever can steal for others, steal.

Blessèd are those who understand, any possession is
an act of theft, just as any love comes from former love.

Blessèd are those who call from full hospital balconies,
Give us your baby, knowing we are all someone's baby.

Blessèd are those who will not wait to be saved, who
swim in the streets, cross the bridge, save us from ourselves.

JESSICA GARRATT

Cogito

The maple outside my window
shakes its big yellow fever at me,
a spot-light in the wind. I'm in bed
reading *First Meditation, Concerning
Things That Can be Doubted,*
from a textbook with a neon *Used* sticker
glued to its spine. My throat
is lemon-peel sore, but luckily, like
Descartes, I'm disturbed by no passions
these days. I'm free
in my peaceful solitude
to draw the quilts up to my chin
and think. Elsewhere, a wail
of tires, the soft crush of metal
on metal on an unseen street
as bumpers furrow like eyebrows.
The storm windows rattle.
Descartes is seated by the fire
in his winter dressing gown, the paper
in his hands bearing the reason
for doubting every belief in his senses'
deceptive creed. For, what if,
right now, he was only his own
dream, haunting the attic
of his true body (naked, fast asleep
between the bed-sheets in another room)?
The fire only a painted fire,
drying on the twin, fluttering canvases
of his eyelids? Descartes is locked
in a vise, a bracket in black
ball-point pen. A boy named Adam
owned this book before I did. He paid
his money, read some

of what he was told to read,
then thrust it back into the world
when the semester was finished
hen-pecking him. Adam didn't like
Descartes. He scrawled insults, all caps,
in the white oblivion of the margins.
The delicate, imagined hem
of Descartes' dressing gown did nothing
to touch him. Instead, he wrote *DICK*
beside the fire scene, the letters large and hard
as the clang of a grate, slammed shut
in a silent room. I can almost see
the tough grudge of his shoulders,
fending off the intrusion of books,
which burden him with the suggestion
that he might not be everything,
or enough. What was this book (dead
on the shelves of cinderblocks and
two-by-fours, lining the blank edge
of his room), compared to what he had suffered
in the space of a single day
when he got dumped, and walked around
like a long, thin paper-cut
before it bleeds? Descartes drew a diagram
of pain, to show how it was separate
from the mind: a resigned, cherub of a man,
one toe dipped in the furled cabbage
of a fire, parting the skin, opening a hollow
extension cord, hooked up to the brain,
for *the animal spirit* to flow through
and inflate the muscle, inviting the leg
to withdraw. Adam withdrew.
But his dreams stuck around like brick
tenements, blocking the view, the sun, his mind
pale, hacking up images
of people and places, gluing them
to 1989, to yesterday, to never,
with a hot, tacking shame that wouldn't dry
evenly, or hold. He woke each morning with half

an erection, aimed at no one, no place
in particular, the constellation of acne scars
on his roommate's back a sign
that nothing mattered, the closed curtains
a shade of green that said the same,
as dim, beer-thin watts of winter light
nudged them, the storm windows rattling.
Descartes recorded only the three
consecutive dreams (plotted clearly
as points on a plane, arcing upward)
that drove him to unearth *the foundation
of the wonderful science.* He was twenty-three
at the time, and had to believe
in a divine destiny, since his father
called René his one disappointment
in life, a son so ridiculous
as to have himself bound in calfskin!
So the son could do nothing
but prove God – a God that made the real
him. His parents were responsible
for his body (that modest, restless curtain
concealing the open window
of his true, immaterial self); there was nothing
he could do about that. Except doubt
everything but what he thought
they could not touch or ruin; nothing to do
except make them not matter, made everything matter
as little as possible, in order to ignore
the other edge of the knife laid down
inside him: hopeful, threatening to try
something new.

STEVE KISTULENTZ

Bargain

The songs that summer spoke only
in the imperative voice, *jump, shout, relax,*
even though everyone knew what a bad idea
it was to demand anything from teenagers.
Besides, we wanted testimony, witness,
to suffer the insufferable and survive;
for my sins, that's exactly
what I got. So when I said *I'd pay*
any price just to win you, I meant Southern
Comfort and ginger, gutwater and iodine,
and twenty years of knowing how sad it is
to be aphastic, another sodden minstrel
speaking of remembered joys,
a naked body I will never again
touch. I preferred more honest bargains,
all the quid pro quos of townhouse basements or
Plymouth backseats or even the 1971 Volkswagen Beetle
I remember with one brown door.
Someday I might want to be a secret again,
kept from someone's mother, and not
the pleasant neighborly boy
she remembers, filed away in the category
of *whatever happened to,* island
of lost luggage. But suppose
we woke up and it was 1985 again;
how would we recognize the death-thin
finger of fate tapping us
on the shoulder unless it pushed
us down into the same
two, back-of-the-bus seats
with their pockmarked burns that smelled
of dry mustard? A secret is
only a secret if it is never told

and this one is nothing
but the memory of negotiations, incidents
and accidents and yes, hints
and allegations, too.
The ghost in you haunts
the theater at the Springfield Mall;
we will never be as close
as the passenger seat, on those mornings
when – brain fried day-glo –
we refused to say good night. Ambiguity,
you said, is best washed away with
five-dollar champagne. We would be lovers
until the missiles were flying, hallelujah,
a promise made before God and Mary
Jane Clement in second period Latin,
unsanctified, useless, forever unfulfilled.
Reagan went to Reykjavik, and we went
to a mythical place called *college,*
where I cannot recall a single thing we did,
except to know I have not, until now,
felt as close to the end
of the world.

This is where they planted the seeds

This is where they planted the seeds
that looked like the tiny white hats
they wore. This is where my back
misses its beat, is stung. This is where
they built the house. This is where I
bled, like the fox they tied to the tree.
This is how they claimed the East. See
how the little fox cries, see how he gives
in to death, a weakling, a fallen soldier. This
is the beach. This is the sand in the shoe
where they infected the wound. This is where
they named this place, poked a flag in the
skin, made us unholy. We are lacking, the
fox and I. We are hanging from a tree.

SARAH LIER

Moonfruit

The first fruit they ate on the moon was a peach.

Maybe it was underripe,
pale as the orb
they had circled for days,
thinking pearls
and milk-bulged breasts, wanting
to stick their teeth in it. They
had dreamed of the way light
came off like a sweater,
not its own. The peach tasted
like that. It was metallic and sour.
Its juice was scanty, sparse
as stars.

Maybe it was ripe
and silk, had the complexion
of roadsigns at night.
They'd been thinking for days
how it would rupture
open, spill sweet. It got into
the roots of their hair,
the taste ruffled through them
like a lifted skirt.
They smacked rosily down
on it, thinking wholeness,
fruit without gravity.

Maybe it was overripe,
collapsing with bog-scented
bruises, the cloy and tang they
recognized, standing on the polyp
of something ancient as a seed, white

as sin. They ate quick,
tonguing the reek, and it slipped
into them like a snake. They left
the pit in the talcum crevices
they'd walked. It would take
two thousand years
to grow.

ANDREW LIPPMAN

To Michael Who I Knew in Fifth Grade

In the suburbs when parents divorce they
marry their friends and so
we became brothers.

Before, my mother
put on your father like clothes:
Slipped an arm here, a chest –

it happened like this. Your mother
was a non-factor. Mine
spoke in smoke rings large as cows' eyes.

Then she shattered the covenant. Shameless
and after the pieces arranged
strangely, with new school relations,

with the hatred I had in my heart. And brother, my mother
has no heart for mending. Watch her a moment:
the tall glass, the pregnant mouth.

DOROTHY ALLEN

For Rachel

In tenth grade, dutiful Jam'iliah hoped to rescue me
Proffering her dog-eared Youth Bible so I knew from what.
Sisyphus, I wanted to call her. I will always be just out of your reach.

Rachel and Ruth. Cream and fire. Ruth's hair the color of redwood,
Rachel's the lightning that blackens it.
Holy women, strong, with gentle hands and venomous tongues.

When I was a child, I thought God only came out
On Christmas. I wasn't sure what he did in the off-season.
I imagined him slumbering like a great bear.

The poor Virgin, last seen in the nineties in a plate glass window –
Even her name turned acronym: Blessed Virgin Mary, or
BVM, for ease and efficiency of prayer.

The church is your home – mother, father, step-father
All pastors – your light hair flashing blue, red, under stained glass.
You taught me to love without dictating what.

Red monuments like overgrown rhubarb stalks
Fasten the vast desert to the sky. Valley of the Gods. O earth,
Something holy like libation blood has soaked into you.

Rachel, what would you have done with this empty sky,
The small tent your tabernacle, the motor running
Beneath you like a large iron heart?

BRIAN CHRISTIAN

The Present

It's good practice. It keeps the flies off,
the phoenixes down. It keeps the butter
soft, the cocksure cock hard. It's a
strengthening agent, toughens you up. It makes
you brittle and/or suffer. It makes you a
man but not in that way. It forces you
to accept a number of contradictory propositions.
Its logic unfolds from invisible axioms.
It produces color, but only as a secondary
quality grounded in texture. It takes up
space, but only as a secondary quality grounded
in color. It folds, unfolds, sags. It
hates you. That's what it does. It folds
you up like a blintz, an origami balloon,
a fortune teller. It plays wastrel to you,
minstrel to you. It puts a head on your
shoulders, knocks it off. It puts hair on your
back, waxes it. It takes your fingerprint
and runs off with it. It takes forever
to get anything done around here. It
takes a lot out of you. It gives you a
headache, a heartache, a hernia. It takes
a village to raise your child, a gurney to
raise your body, courage to raise your
voice. It's a membrane between all
that there is and nothing. It cost me
a fortune so I hope you like it.

LAURA DAVENPORT

Black & White of James Dean

In what would be green lawn, he holds
A gray leaf –
Cross-legged, counting the tulip poplar's
Small veins,
dark threads, each line on his face
drawn downward, in what appears to be
Spring – The moment is private.
Still, a camera –
Beside him, his co-star sweeps back
The dark hair from her forehead:
Liz Taylor, beaming,
watches and smokes,
The space between them
Lit, exposure
Whitening the dappled grass.
As if to say
Celebrities, too, count blossoms,
He looks down at the lawn
And frowns.
Cuffs pressed, his collar curves
Beautifully, closed over his chest
With a dark button.
Oh, Jim! These days,
Fresh deaths
Eclipse each other with newer,
Better angles: by fire,
By water, by speed,
Held-down
Desires. In the still afternoon, a break
Between takes, what do you say
To her? Aware of the camera,
Muttering, perhaps,
An escape. Do you wish

For a smaller soul,
One the world will not be sore at you
For taking?
This is the set of your last
Movie. And watching now, you look
So tired, Jim.
But I do not think
You know that. Rather than determine
Who will receive your wristwatch with black
Band, gold-plated cigarette
Lighter, you are thinking
About leaves – What kind
Are they? Why have you never
Studied them?

Fun House Mirror

Inside the photo our arms grow long again, Mother
you are stooped, your face shorter, turned into
my shoulder, your laugh curled into the yellow

raincoat. The lines beginning to show across
your forehead, how you were soft on most days,
the migraines, drawing all of the shades, now

why do we bulge inward, back into the vermillion
kitchen, peach-warm hand prying open my mouth,
for what I've taken, scarf fallen revealing your shorn

head, a fence line of stitches bleeding into the scene,
wicker chair sighing its aches saying to me young *we have to
get there before it gets dark,* to the fair, and now to the back

porch where you smoked new menthols this past weekend
on my short trip home, your son watching through
the screen, eleven, and trying to cover my eyes before

I came to see you so changed, the smoke hanging out
of your mouth while we drove around like restless girls,
the gas light on for miles, the house falling apart, out

of your sight, the IRS on our tail the whole time, *the gut
it must have took* to look at me and ask for cash so much
so you had to nap, the dogs dragging mud across

your chest, my hand wound around your thumb,
where another cyst has come to rest –

The Very Hungry Caterpillar dropped on the bed, by your
grandson, Aidan, open to the pages where holes have

been eaten through all the fruit, the page that scares

him, and he sticks his finger in saying *holes,* burying
his face in your robe, knowing nothing of the fist that
settled into your head and bloomed when I was thirteen,

watching as storms appeared, small plums along your arm
where the needle knew more of you than I did, how you
swayed back and forth, trying to figure out if it was affordable

to be removed, quieting the men behind as the camera
catches a woman's waist off to one side, red and belted,
you saying into my neck *look at us, look at us.*

STEVE TOUSSAINT

My Left, Your Right

I wangled in a field of rotundas.
The band played "Moonshiner"
on lyres made of coral.
Eunuchs fled the harem for Denver.
Everyone westernized.
It was the year of the gherkin.
County fairs spread like an orchid epidemic.
The out-of-towners drained their lesions
at the truckstop.
A radish pinked the filly's gums.
Uncle Remus lit his beard on fire with a taper.
He told the story of Saint Gus and the concubine
to a campload of frightened children.
Not soup enough to feed the urchins
but ten delicious steaks
in the horse I'll build someday.
I run a hand over my moles.
Two moles. On my back.

AARON WHEETLEY

Obsidian Creek

Blackened forest. I am looking at photography of Yellowstone
circa probably nineteen eighty-eight, after it burned.
A bull elk pauses to mull over the wildfire's reclamation
mid-stride fallen lodgepole pine. If I had a thimbleful
of that resolve it might make a nice metaphor
for the end of my marriage. The fire,
the stopping there, and then the clear exhalation
of vapor like an offering
before the clean, burnt forest.
The bull elk, according to the caption, is *bugling.*
So there, in the ashen and quicksilver interlace
of fallen trunk-work
he means to wolf inamoratas
while he trucks with the landscape.
I think I understand some of his meaning
in the same way listeners can fall under the spell
of a Wagner opera, or commuters, on the el
platform, can find themselves swept up
in the sheer bracing pressure, sounds,
of the pop and the hiss of the rails and the wheels
without really comprehending the language or the reason.
The elk's migrating too, urged along by his stomach
and his harem, his hooves split
serotinous seeds. And behind him,
his twelve-points, the branches and the trunks fade
into an infinite regression
as if the fire has hollowed them, finally,
and sent them all looking inward.

Notes on the Contributors

DOROTHY ALLEN grew up in the woods just outside Durham, North Carolina, and wrote her first poems about the small brown creek in her family's backyard. She now lives in Vermont, where she studies literature and printmaking at Bennington College. She will graduate in June 2009.

FRANCISCO ARAGÓN is the author of the poetry collection *Puerta del Sol* (Bilingual Press, 2005) and editor of the award-winning anthology *The Wind Shifts: New Latino Poetry* (University of Arizona Press, 2007). He is director of Letras Latinas – the literary program of the Institute for Latino Studies at the University of Notre Dame. For more information, visit www.franciscoaragon.net.

MEG ARENBERG received her B.A. in creative writing and environmental studies from Oberlin College in 2001. Since that time she has pursued myriad academic and professional adventures, the latest of which led her to New Haven, Connecticut. Meg recently returned to writing projects and is currently at work translating a novel from Swahili.

CYNTHIA ARRIEU-KING is assistant professor of creative writing at Stockton College and an echocardiographer. Her poems and reviews have appeared in *Prairie Schooner, Jacket, New Orleans Review, Black Warrior Review, Forklift, Ohio,* and others. A Kundiman fellow, she received an honorable mention from John Yau for her chapbook *The Small Anything City,* which won the 2006 Dream Horse Press National Chapbook Competition.

JAMES ARTHUR's poems have appeared or are forthcoming in *The New Yorker, The New Republic, The Antioch Review,* and *The Southern Review.* He has received the Amy Lowell Traveling Poetry Scholarship, a Discovery/ *The Nation* Prize, and a Stegner Fellowship, as well as fellowships to Yaddo and the MacDowell Colony. He lives in Oakland with his wife, fiction writer Shannon Robinson.

WILLIAM S. BARNES is a botanist, ecologist, and science teacher in Santa Fe, New Mexico. In 1998 and 1999, he was awarded the Academy of American Poets Prize while studying for his master's in biology. He has recent poems in the *CutBank Review* and the *Eleventh Muse* and has just completed a new manuscript. He is most interested in the intersections of language and place.

CHLOE BARNETT graduated from Bryn Mawr College in 2006. After spending a year as a curatorial intern at the Dallas Museum of Art, she entered the master's program in art history at the University of Texas at Austin. In the fall of 2009, she hopes to begin studies in rare book and special collections librarianship.

TERRI K. BORCHERS, associate professor of humanities and director of professional writing at Medaille College, teaches poetry, literature, creative expression, and advanced writing classes. She has published and presented articles on Elizabeth Bishop, Toi Derricotte, and the problematics of we. Her poems have appeared in several leading journals, and she has worked as advisor to the national award-winning Medaille College creative arts journal, the *Prelude*.

NICOLE BRODSKY lives in San Francisco, teaches at San Francisco State University and the University of San Francisco, and plays in two bands: The Size Queens and Apopka Darkroom.

GABRIELLE CALVOCORESSI's awards include a Stegner Fellowship in Poetry, a Jones Lectureship in Poetry at Stanford University, a Rona Jaffe Writers' Award, and *The Paris Review*'s Bernard F. Conners Prize. Her first collection, *The Last Time I Saw Amelia Earhart* (Persea Books, 2005), won the Connecticut Book Award. Her second collection, *Apocalyptic Swing*, is forthcoming from Persea Books. She lives in Los Angeles and teaches in the M.F.A. programs at both California College of Arts in San Francisco and Warren Wilson College.

JENNIFER CHANG's first book, *The History of Anonymity*, was an inaugural selection of the *VQR* Poetry Series and was published by the University of Georgia Press in 2008. She has received fellowships from the MacDowell Colony and Yaddo, and her poems have appeared in *Boston Review, Kenyon Review, New England Review, The New Republic*, and *A Public Space*.

BRIAN CHRISTIAN's poems and essays appear in *AGNI, Gulf Coast, Seneca Review, Ninth Letter*, and *Best New Poets*, and on the Web at *Conjunctions* and *McSweeney's*. Born in Wilmington, Delaware, Christian holds degrees in computer science, philosophy, and poetry from Brown University and the University of Washington. He lives in Seattle.

WENDY COULTER lives and works in Tucson, Arizona. She holds advanced degrees in poetry and creative nonfiction and is a certified yoga instructor. Her work has been published in journals including *South Dakota Review, Natural Bridge, Half Tones to Jubilee*, and *SunDog*. She has also served as production editor, poetry editor, and editor-in-chief of *Sonora Review*.

LAURA DAVENPORT hails from Birmingham, Alabama. She is currently an M.F.A. candidate at Virginia Commonwealth University.

KIRK LEE DAVIS has taught at the University of Michigan and the University of Wisconsin, where he served as Jay C. and Ruth Halls Poetry Fellow. He is currently a member of the Hampshire School of Art.

ERICA DAWSON's collection, *Big-Eyed Afraid* (Waywiser, 2007), won the 2006 Anthony Hecht Poetry Prize. Her poems have appeared or are forthcoming in *Virginia Quarterly Review*, *Harvard Review*, and other journals and have appeared in anthologies, including *Best American Poetry 2008*. She lives in Cincinnati, Ohio, where she is pursuing a Ph.D. in English literature.

RACHEL DEWOSKIN is the author of *Foreign Babes in Beijing* (Norton, 2005), which has been published in six countries and is being developed as a feature film by Paramount. Her novel, *Repeat After Me*, is forthcoming in 2009. She has published poetry in various journals, including *Ploughshares*, *Seneca Review*, *The New Delta Review*, and *Nerve*. She teaches creative writing at NYU.

BEN DOLLER's first book, *Radio, Radio* (Louisiana State University Press, 2001), won the 2000 Walt Whitman Award under the name Ben Doyle. His second book, *FAQ:*, was published in 2009 by Ahsahta Press, and his third, *Dead Ahead*, will appear from Fence Books in 2010. He lives in San Diego with his wife, the poet Sandra Doller, and teaches at the University of California, San Diego.

MOLLY DOWD is originally from Fairfield, Pennsylvania. She recently earned an M.F.A. in creative writing from the University of Alabama, where she served as editor of the *Black Warrior Review*. Her poems have appeared in *Crab Creek Review*.

JEHANNE DUBROW's work has appeared in *Poetry*, *The Hudson Review*, *New England Review*, *Shenandoah*, and *Gulf Coast*. She is the author of a poetry collection, *The Hardship Post* (Three Candles Press, 2009) and a chapbook, *The Promised Bride* (Finishing Line Press, 2007).

Poetry was a hobby casualty for JOHN ERHARDT in 2003, shortly after he graduated from the University of Massachusetts with his M.F.A. Instead, he began writing about baseball and contributed to the 2006 and 2007 editions of the *Baseball Prospectus* annual (Penguin) and to *It Ain't Over 'Til It's Over: The Baseball Prospectus Race Book* (Basic Books, 2007). He now works as a technical writer and builds furniture with 19th-century hand tools.

NAVA ETSHALOM learned to talk in Jerusalem and to read in Brooklyn. Now she's a Philadelphia-based poet and essayist. She was a 2006 Pew Fellow in the Arts; her poems have appeared recently in *FIELD*, *Meridian*, and *Mid-American Review*. She has a B.A. from Oberlin College and an M.F.A. in poetry from the University of Michigan.

KATIE FORD is the author of *Deposition* (2002) and *Colosseum* (2008), both published by Graywolf Press. *Colosseum* was named a Best Book of the year by *Publishers Weekly*. She is the recipient of a 2008 Lannan Literary Award and lives in Philadelphia with her husband.

EVA FOSTER is a Ph.D. student in creative writing at the University of Houston. She earned an M.F.A. from the University of Maryland. She was a winner of the Academy of American Poets College Prize and the Jane Marie Luecke Prize for Poetry as well as a fellowship from Inprint Houston.

MARGARET FUNKHOUSER's poems have appeared in several publications, including the *Boston Review* and *The Paris Review*. She lives in Natick, Massachusetts.

RACHEL GALVIN was a Michener Fellow at the University of Texas at Austin and is currently a Ph.D. candidate in the Department of Comparative Literature at Princeton University. Her poems and translations appear in *Drunken Boat*, *Gulf Coast*, and *McSweeney's*. She is the author of a chapbook of poems, *Zoetrope* (Ediciones Chätaro, 2006). Her first book of poems, *Pulleys & Locomotion*, was published in 2009 by Black Lawrence Press.

NATHAN GAMACHE lives outside Boston, Massachusetts. Send him some poems at nathan.gamache@yahoo.com.

JESSICA GARRATT grew up in Maryland and is currently a doctoral candidate and Creative Writing Fellow at the University of Missouri. Her first book, *Fire Pond*, was awarded the 2008 Agha Shahid Ali Prize in Poetry and published by the University of Utah Press. Individual poems have appeared in a number of journals, including *Michigan Quarterly Review*, *Shenandoah*, and *North American Review*.

LIANA HOLMBERG is an accidental poet. She also writes fiction, journalism, and quarterly reports. Liana grew up in a rural town in Hawaii and now lives in San Francisco, where she works for the online virtual world Second Life. High tech is full of great stories, but she sometimes misses tropical rain pounding against a corrugated tin roof.

ANN HUNKINS is an award-winning poet, photographer, and translator of Nepali. A former Fulbright scholar with an M.A. in poetry from UC-Davis, she is currently translating a Nepali novel into English on an N.E.A. translation grant. She worked as an interpreter for the United Nations in Nepal during the Maoist conflict. She writes and milks goats in Santa Fe, New Mexico.

SHANLEY JACOBS is an M.F.A. candidate at Virginia Commonwealth University. In 2008, she received the Academy of American Poets Catherine and Joan Byrne College Poetry Prize. She has poems forthcoming in *Gulf Coast*.

ANNA JOURNEY is the author of *If Birds Gather Your Hair for Nesting* (University of Georgia Press, 2009), winner of the National Poetry Series. She's currently a Ph.D. candidate in creative writing and literature at the University of Houston and a poetry editor for *Gulf Coast*.

AMY E. KING earned a B.A. from Bryn Mawr College, an M.F.A. from Emerson College, and an M.L.S. from Syracuse University. She and her wife live in Massachusetts.

STEVE KISTULENTZ is a two-time winner of the Academy of American Poets John Mackay Shaw Prize. He is a doctoral candidate at Florida State University, where he holds the Edward and Marie Kingsbury Fellowship. His work has appeared in *Best New Poets 2008* and such literary magazines as the *Antioch, Black Warrior, Crab Orchard,* and *New England Reviews; Caesura; New Letters; Quarterly West;* and many others.

CHRISTINE LARUSSO is a Fordham graduate and California native now residing and writing in Brooklyn, New York. This is her first published poem.

BRIAN LEARY is the managing editor of *420pus,* an online journal of the literary arts. He lives in Brooklyn.

ALEX LEMON is the author of *Mosquito* (Tin House Books, 2006), *Hallelujah Blackout* (Milkweed Editions, 2008), and the memoir *Happy* (Scribner, 2009).

JONAS LERMAN is a law student at UC-Berkeley and the editor-in-chief of the *California Law Review.* His poems have appeared in *Crazyhorse, Indiana Review, Lyric, Mid-American Review, Permafrost, Poetry Daily, Puerto del Sol,* and elsewhere. His Web site is jonaslerman.com.

SARAH LIER's poetry has appeared in *Inkwell, The Sow's Ear,* and *So to Speak.* She plays the mandolin in her Brooklyn-based band, the Sugar Tulips. She's working on two novel-length stories: one about the difficulties of looking for otherworlds in modern America, the other about her recurring dreams set in an abandoned version of New York City. She currently lives in New Jersey.

ANDREW LIPPMAN is a senior English major at Grinnell College. He currently lives in East Rockaway, New York.

MOLLY LUBY received her M.F.A. in writing from UNC-Greensboro in 2000. She currently teaches English and humanities at Central Carolina Community College in Sanford, North Carolina, where she also serves as editor for *The Red Clay Review.*

CATE MARVIN is the author of two poetry collections, *World's Tallest Disaster* (2001) and *Fragment of the Head of the Queen* (2007), and co-editor with the poet Michael Dumanis of the anthology *Legitimate Dangers* (2006), all of which were published by Sarabande Books. An associate professor in creative writing at the College of Staten Island CUNY, she is a recipient of the Kate Tufts Discovery Prize and a Whiting Award.

ROSALIE METRO has taught history and English in the Bronx and on the Thailand-Burma border. She is now working on a Ph.D. in education at Cornell University and is also looking to publish her first novel. She lives with her husband in Columbia, Missouri.

SEAN NEVIN is the author of *Oblivio Gate* (Southern Illinois University Press, 2008), which won the Crab Orchard Series First Book Award, and *A House that Falls*, winner of the Slapering Hol Press Chapbook Prize in 2005. His honors include the Robinson Jeffers Tor House Prize for Poetry and a Literature Fellowship in Poetry from the National Endowment for the Arts.

MIHO NONAKA is a bilingual writer from Tokyo. Her first book, *Garasu no tsuki*, was a finalist for Japan's national poetry prize. Her poems and nonfiction have appeared or are forthcoming in *Crab Orchard Review, Iowa Review, The Spoon River Poetry Review*, and *Satellite Convulsions: Poems from Tin House*, among others. She teaches English at Eastern Illinois University.

JILL OSIER grew up in northeastern Iowa and studied at Luther College and the University of Alaska-Fairbanks. Her work has been awarded a National Endowment for the Arts Fellowship and the Diane Middlebrook Fellowship (UW-Madison). Some of her poems can be found in *Black Warrior Review, Crazyhorse, The Gettysburg Review, Poetry, Prairie Schooner*, and *32 Poems*.

ROBERT OSTROM's work has appeared or is forthcoming in *Drunken Boat, Glitterpony, 42opus, Western Humanities Review*, and elsewhere. His chapbook, *To Show the Living*, won the 2008 Center for Book Arts Chapbook Competition. He lives in Brooklyn.

JULIE SOPHIA PAEGLE's poetry has appeared or is forthcoming in *Best New Poets, Writers on the California Deserts, Ploughshares, Prairie Schooner, The Iowa Review, The Southern Review, Aplinist, Colorado Review, Denver Quarterly*, and others. She teaches creative writing and literature at California State University-San Bernardino and lives in the San Bernardino Mountains with her husband and sons.

MICHAEL PICKARD graduated from Millsaps College and received a master's in creative writing from Boston University. The 2005–06 Writer-in-Residence at St. Albans School in Washington, D.C., he is currently a Ph.D. candidate at the University of Virginia.

YOSEFA RAZ's poems, stories, and translations have appeared in *ZYZZYVA, Glimmer Train*, and *Tikkun*, among other venues. *In Exchange for a Homeland*, a poetry book, was published by Swan Scythe Press in 2004. Raz is currently a Ph.D. candidate at UC-Berkeley, studying Biblical prophetic poetry and its Hebrew Modernist revisions.

ELIZABETH RISTOW has studied poetry with Sally Keith, James Longenbach, and Karen Subach, and fiction with Joanna Scott. She holds bachelor's and master's degrees from the Eastman School of Music in viola performance and music education. She lives with her husband in Rochester, New York, where she plays and teaches.

SPENCER SHORT was born in Elkton, Maryland, in 1972. His first collection, *Tremolo*, won the 2000 National Poetry Series competition and was published in 2001 by HarperCollins. He lives in Brooklyn, New York.

JERROLD SHIROMA was born and raised in San Diego, California. He received his B.A. from San Francisco State University in 2000 and an M.F.A. from Brown University in 2003. Since 1999, he has been the editor/publisher of duration press and durationpress.com.

A native of Columbus, Ohio, MAGGIE SMITH holds an M.F.A. from Ohio State University. Her first collection of poetry, *Lamp of the Body* (2005), won the Benjamin Saltman Award and was published by Red Hen Press. Smith's poems have appeared or are forthcoming in *The Paris Review, The Gettysburg Review, Indiana Review, Gulf Coast, The Iowa Review*, and elsewhere.

KRISTINE SOMERVILLE works at *The Missouri Review* as the marketing coordinator and teaches creative nonfiction, fiction, and literary studies at Stephens College. Her short stories, nonfiction, and prose poems have appeared in *The North American Review, Hayden's Ferry, Passages North, Quarterly West*, and elsewhere. Her essay "Katie Suber" received a notable mention in *Best American Essays 2000*, and her fiction has been nominated twice for a Pushcart Prize. Her visual and "found text" features appear regularly in *The Missouri Review*.

STEVE TOUSSAINT was born and raised in Chicago, where he attended Loyola University as an undergraduate. He is currently an M.F.A. candidate at the Iowa Writer's Workshop. His poems have appeared or are forthcoming in journals such as *Spires* and *Forklift, Ohio*.

ANDY TREBING works in Chicago, where he lives with a lady, a cat, and a dog called Chickenwing. He holds an M.F.A. in poetry from Columbia College, Chicago, and his poems have appeared in *Mipoesias, Arsenic Lobster*, and *The Concher*.

JILL TREMBLAY worked as a writer for an association before deciding to make a big leap into teaching. After completing a one-year master's program at George Washington University, Jill is anxiously awaiting her first year teaching at an elementary school in the D.C.-metro area. She promises to inspire a love of poetry in all of her students.

KATIE UMANS has published poems in *Indiana Review, Barrow Street, Crazyhorse, The Bellingham Review, Beloit Poetry Journal, Court Green, Forklift, Ohio,* and others. In 2005 and 2006, she was Jay C. and Ruth Halls Poetry Fellow at the University of Wisconsin, Madison. She now lives in New Hampshire.

JENNIFER J. UNDERSTAHL received her B.F.A. in poetry from the University of Evansville in 1995, her M.F.A. in poetry from Arizona State University in 2000, and her J.D. from Vanderbilt University Law School in 2005. She currently lives in Phoenix, Arizona, and makes money to feed and clothe her three daughters by masquerading as a real estate attorney.

SARAH VAP is the author of *American Spikenard,* winner of the 2006 Iowa Poetry Prize, and *Dummy Fire,* winner of the 2006 Saturnalia Poetry Prize. Her third collection, *Faulkner's Rosary,* is forthcoming from Saturnalia Books. She lives on the Olympic Peninsula with her family and is the poetry editor at *420pus.*

ELLEN VINZ is a first-year law student at the University of Wisconsin.

MILES WAGGENER is the author of *Phoenix Suites* (The Word Works, 2003), winner of the Washington Prize, and a chapbook, *Portents Aside* (Two Dogs Press, 2008). A graduate of the University of Montana and recipient of the Richard Hugo Memorial Scholarship, Waggener recently joined the writing faculty of University of Nebraska at Omaha. He lives with his wife and fellow poet, Megan Gannon.

DAVID WELCH has poems published or forthcoming in several journals, including *Pleiades, Ninth Letter,* and *The Laurel Review.* He received his M.F.A. from the University of Alabama and currently lives in Chicago.

AARON WHEETLEY is finishing an M.F.A. in creative writing at Southern Illinois University at Carbondale.

JERRY WILLIAMS teaches at Marymount Manhattan College and lives in the Bronx. Carnegie Mellon University Press published his first collection of poems, *Casino of the Sun,* in 2003, and will publish his second, *Admission,* in 2010. He also edited the anthology *It's Not You, It's Me: The Poetry of Breakup and Divorce,* forthcoming from Overlook Press in 2010.

ANNA ZIEGLER's plays have been produced off-Broadway in New York and in London. Her poems have appeared in *The Best American Poetry 2003, The Threepenny Review, The Michigan Quarterly Review, The Mississippi Review, Arts and Letters, Mid-American Review, Smartish Pace, The Saint Ann's Review,* and other journals. For more information, please see www.annabziegler.com.

Acknowledgments

The following poems were reprinted with permission from the poet and publisher. All rights reserved.

Francisco Aragón, "Jugglers": from *Light, Yogurt, Strawberry Milk*, published by Chicano Chapbook Series, 1999, edited by Gary Soto. Copyright © 1999 by Francisco Aragón.

Gabrielle Calvocoressi, "Graves We Filled Before the Fire": from *The Last Time I Saw Amelia Earhart*, published by Persea Books, 2005. Copyright © 2005 by Gabrielle Calvocoressi.

Brian Christian, "The Present": from *Best New Poets 2008*, edited by Mark Strand and Jeb Livingood, published by Samovar Press, 2008. Copyright © 2008 by Brian Christian.

Wendy Coulter, "Winnowing": originally appeared in *South Dakota Review,* 1999. Copyright © 1999 by Wendy Coulter.

Kirk Lee Davis, "In the Greenroom: The Rhyming Couple": originally appeared in *The Concher,* Issue II, 2009. Copyright © 2009 by Kirk Lee Davis.

Erica Dawson, "Semantics": from *Big Eyed Afraid,* published by The Waywiser Press, 2007. Copyright © 2007 by Erica Dawson.

Rachel DeWoskin, "Love Poem from South China, 1999": originally appeared in *Seneca Review,* Spring 2000. Copyright © 2009 by Rachel DeWoskin.

Ben Doller, "Radio, Radio": from *Radio, Radio*, published by Louisiana State University Press, 2001. Copyright © 2001 by Ben Doyle.

Jehanne Dubrow, "Milosz on All Saints Day": from *The Hardship Post,* published by Three Candles Press, 2009. Copyright © 2009 by Jehanne Dubrow.

Nava EtShalom, "Places to Put Your Body": originally appeared in *Mid-American Review*, 2005. Copyright © 2005 by Nava EtShalom.

Margaret Funkhouser, "Crown": originally appeared in *The Paris Review,* Spring 2004. Copyright © 2004 by Margaret Funkhouser.

Rachel Galvin, "Letter Spoken in Wind": from *Pulleys & Locomotion*, published by Black Lawrence Press, 2009. Copyright © 2009 by Rachel Galvin.

Jessica Garratt, "Cogito": from *Fire Pond*, published by University of Utah Press, 2009. Copyright © 2009 by Jessica Garratt. Originally appeared in *Michigan Quarterly Review* 47.1, 2008.

Alex Lemon, "Mosquito": from *Mosquito*, published by Tin House Books, 1996. Copyright © 1996 by Alex Lemon.

Jonas Lerman, "Your Grandmother": originally appeared in *Lewis & Clark Review,* 2003. Copyright © 2003 by Jonas Lerman.

Index of Poets and Judges

Participating Colleges and Prizes

AGNES SCOTT COLLEGE
Janef Preston Poetry Prize
Donor: Agnes Scott College

AMHERST COLLEGE
Academy of American Poets Prize
Donor: Amherst College

AQUINAS COLLEGE
Academy of American Poets Prize
Donor: Linda Nemec Foster

ARIZONA STATE UNIVERSITY
Katharine C. Turner Prize
Donor: Katharine C. Turner

AUBURN UNIVERSITY
Robert Hughes Mount Jr. Prize in Poetry
Donor: Mrs. Frances Mayes

AUGSBURG COLLEGE
John R. Mitchell Academy of American
Poets Prize
Donor: Mrs. Jeanette Mitchell

BARD COLLEGE
The Flow Chart Foundation / Academy
of American Poets Prize
Donor: David Kermani

BAYLOR UNIVERSITY
Academy of American Poets Prize
Donor: Beall Poetry Festival

BELOIT COLLEGE
Beloit Poetry Journal Prize
Donor: Marion Stocking

BENNINGTON COLLEGE
The Green Prize for Poetry
Donors: Ms. Kelly Green & Mr. Forrest
MacGregor

BLOOMSBURG UNIVERSITY
Richard Savage Poetry Award
Donor: Bloomsburg University

BOSTON UNIVERSITY
Academy of American Poets Prize
Donor: Boston University Creative
Writing Program

BOWDOIN COLLEGE
Academy of American Poets Prize
Donor: Bowdoin College

BRADLEY UNIVERSITY
Sipple Poetry Prize
Donor: John B. Shorrock

BRANDEIS UNIVERSITY
The Ramon Feliciano Poetry Prize
Donor: Marion McDonald

BRIGHAM YOUNG UNIVERSITY
Ethel Lowry Handley Poetry Prize
Donor: Ethel Lowry Handley

BROOKLYN COLLEGE, CUNY
Burton A. Goldberg Poetry Prize
Donor: Burton Goldberg

BROWN UNIVERSITY
The Academy of American Poets Prize
Donor: Leander McCormick-Goodhart

BRYN MAWR COLLEGE
Prize in Memory of Marie Bullock
Donor: Peter McCormick

**CALIFORNIA POLYTECHNIC STATE
UNIVERSITY**
Academy of American Poets Prize
Donor: California Polytechnic State
University

**CALIFORNIA STATE UNIVERSITY,
FRESNO**
Larry Levis Memorial Poetry Prize
Donors: Frances & Philip Levine

**CALIFORNIA STATE UNIVERSITY,
FRESNO**
Ernesto Trejo Memorial Prize
Donor: Jon Veinberg

**CALIFORNIA STATE UNIVERSITY,
LOS ANGELES**
Henri Coulette Memorial Award
Donor: California State University, Los
Angeles

**CALIFORNIA STATE UNIVERSITY,
NORTHRIDGE**
George Dillon Memorial Award
Donor: Jean Burden

CALVIN COLLEGE
The Academy of American Poets Prize
Donor: Calvin College

CARNEGIE MELLON UNIVERSITY
Academy of American Poets Prize
Donor: Carnegie Mellon University

CENTRAL PENNSYLVANIA COLLEGE
Geraldine G. Britcher Poetry Prize
Donor: Raymond W. Britcher

CENTRE COLLEGE
Paul Cantrell Poetry Prize
Donor: Phillip Sterling

CHATHAM UNIVERSITY
The Laurie Mansell Reich Poetry Prize
Donor: Laurie and Henry Reich

CITY COLLEGE OF NEW YORK
Academy of American Poets Prize
Donor: Michal Dekal

CITY COLLEGE OF SAN FRANCISCO
Felicia Farr Lemmon Poetry Prize
Donor: Felicia Farr Lemmon

CLEVELAND STATE UNIVERSITY
Alberta Turner Poetry Prize
Donor: Cleveland State University

COLLEGE OF THE HOLY CROSS
Dominick Lepore Poetry Award
Donor: Dominick J. Lepore

COLLEGE OF WILLIAM AND MARY
Academy of American Poets Prize
Donor: Carolyn Kreiter-Foronda

COLLEGE OF WOOSTER
Cora Owlett Latzer Award
Donor: Susan W. Donnell

COLORADO STATE UNIVERSITY
Academy of American Poets Prize
Donor: Colorado State University Faculty
& Administration

COLUMBIA COLLEGE CHICAGO
Eileen Lannan Poetry Prize
Donor: John R. Lannan

**COLUMBIA UNIVERSITY
(UNDERGRATUATE)**
Academy of American Poets Prize
Donor: Academy of American Poets

COLUMBIA UNIVERSITY (GRADUATE)
Bennett Poetry Prize
Donor: The New York Times Advertising
Department

CONNECTICUT COLLEGE
Charles B. Palmer Poetry Award
Donor: Charles B. Palmer Poetry Award

COOPER UNION
Elizabeth Kray Prize
Donor: Cooper Union

CORNELL COLLEGE
Prize in Memory of Clyde and Jewell
Bothwell Tull
Donor: Alice Louise Haug

CORNELL UNIVERSITY
Academy of American Poets Prize Arthur
Litowitz
Donor: Litowitz Foundation, Inc.

CREIGHTON UNIVERSITY
Donor: Oscar M. Macellaio Poetry Prize
Donor: Mary M. Plauché

DARTMOUTH COLLEGE
Academy of American Poets Prize
Donor: Dartmouth College

DICKINSON COLLEGE
Academy of American Poets Prize
Donor: Dickinson College

DREW UNIVERSITY
Academy of American Poets Prize
Donor: Susan Vartanian Barba

DUKE UNIVERSITY
Academy of American Poets Prize
Donor: The Biddle Foundation

EMERSON COLLEGE
Academy of American Poets Prize
Donor: Emerson College

EMORY UNIVERSITY
Academy of American Poets Prize
Donor: The Friends of Creative Writing

**FLORIDA INTERNATIONAL
UNIVERSITY**
Christopher F. Kelly Award for Poetry
Donor: John Bond

FLORIDA STATE UNIVERSITY
John Mackay Shaw Award for
Undergraduate Poets
Donor: Sandy Crum

125

FLORIDA STATE UNIVERSITY
Academy of American Poets Prize
Donor: Sandy Crum

FORDHAM UNIVERSITY
Academy of American Poets Prize
Donor: Special

FRANKLIN & MARSHALL COLLEGE
Academy of American Poets Prize
Donor: C. Hunter Boll

GEORGE MASON UNIVERSITY
The Joseph A. Lohman III Poetry Prize
Donor: Judith Lelchook

GEORGE WASHINGTON UNIVERSITY
A. E. Claeyssens, Jr. Poetry Prize
Donor: The George Washington
University

GEORGETOWN UNIVERSITY
Ora Mary Phelam Poetry Prize
Donor: J. Patrick Lannan

**GEORGIA COLLEGE & STATE
UNIVERSITY**
Frankye Davis Mayes Prize
Donor: Frances Mayes

GEORGIA PERIMETER COLLEGE
Academy of American Poets Prize
Donor: Lawrence Hetrick

GETTYSBURG COLLEGE
Marion Zulauf Prize
Donor: Sander Zulauf

GRINNELL COLLEGE
Prize in Memory of Lorabel Richardson
Donor: Alice Louise Haug

HAMILTON COLLEGE
Ralph and Doris Hansmann Poetry Prize
Donor: Phillip Blumberg

**HARRISBURG AREA COMMUNITY
COLLEGE**
Dale T. Guhl Memorial Prize
Donor: Raymond W. Britcher

HARTWICK COLLEGE
Anna Sonder Prize
Donor: Otto Sonder

HARVARD UNIVERSITY
Academy of American Poets Prize
Donor: Harvard University

HAVERFORD COLLEGE
James C. Ransom Poetry Prize
Donors: James Haglund & Jason Fritz

HOFSTRA UNIVERSITY
Nancy P. Schnader Award
Donor: Hofstra University

HOLLINS UNIVERSITY
Gertrude Claytor Poetry Prize
Donor: Mr. W. Graham Claytor, Jr.

HOPE COLLEGE
Academy of American Poets Prize
Donor: Hope College

HUNTER COLLEGE
Catalina Pàez & Seumas MacManus
Award
Donors: Mariquita M. Mullan &
Patricia MacManus

ILLINOIS COLLEGE
Academy of American Poets Prize
Donor: Deborah Klang Smith

ILLINOIS WESLEYAN UNIVERSITY
Arthur W. Hinners & Louise Hinners
Sipfle Prize
Donor: David A. Sipfle

INDIANA STATE UNIVERSITY
Madelyn DeGaetano Memorial Poetry Prize
Donor: Elaine L. Kleiner

INDIANA UNIVERSITY
The Vera Meyer Strube Poetry Prize
Donor: Jean Meyer Aloe

KEAN UNIVERSITY OF NEW JERSEY
Kean University Poetry Prize
Donor: Mr. William Kurry

KENYON COLLEGE
Academy of American Poets Prize
Donor: Kenyon College

KEYSTONE COLLEGE
Edward M. Cameron IV Poetry Prize
Donor: Robert D. Corrie

LAFAYETTE COLLEGE
Jean E. Corrie Poetry Prize
Donor: Robert D. Corrie

LEWIS & CLARK COLLEGE
Academy of American Poets Prize
Donor: Lewis & Clark College

**LONG ISLAND UNIVERSITY, C.W.
POST CAMPUS**
John & Agnes McCarten Memorial Award
Donor: Jeanne Marie Scott

LOYOLA UNIVERSITY MARYLAND
Academy of American Poets Prize
Donor: Loyola College

LOYOLA UNIVERSITY OF CHICAGO
Dr. Frank C. Lawler Poetry Prize
Donor: Frank Lawler, Jr.

MACALESTER COLLEGE
Academy of American Poets Prize
Donor: Macalester College

MARIETTA COLLEGE
Stephen Schwartz Prize in Poetry
Donor: Laura Baudo Sillerman

MESSIAH COLLEGE
Carrie A. Guhl Poetry Prize
Donor: Raymond W. Britcher

MIAMI UNIVERSITY (GRADUATE)
Betty Jane Abrahams Memorial Poetry Prize
Donor: Jeffrey Abrahams

MIAMI UNIVERSITY (UNDERGRADUATE)
Harris S. Abrahams Poetry Prize
Donor: Jeffrey Abrahams

MIAMI-DADE COMMUNITY COLLEGE
Fred Shaw Poetry Prize
Donor: Miami-Dade Community College

MOUNT HOLYOKE COLLEGE
Gertrude Claytor Poetry Prize
Donor: F. Murray Claytor

MUHLENBERG COLLEGE
Charles L. Killeen II Poetry Prize
Donor: Charles Killeen

MUSKINGUM COLLEGE
Beulah Brooks Brown Award in Poetry
Donor: Muskingum College

NEW JERSEY CITY UNIVERSITY
The Walter Glospie Academy of
American Poets Prize
Donor: New Jersey City University

NEW MEXICO STATE UNIVERSITY
The Ruth Scott Poetry Award
Donor: Judith N. Scott

NORTH CAROLINA STATE UNIVERSITY
Academy of American Poets Prize
Donor: North Carolina State

NORTHEAST OHIO MASTER IN FINE ARTS
Academy of American Poets Prize
Donor: NOEMFA

NORTHWESTERN UNIVERSITY
Jean Meyer Aloe Poetry Prize
Donor: Jean Meyer Aloe

OBERLIN COLLEGE
Stuart Friebert Poetry Prize
Donor: Oberlin College

OHIO STATE UNIVERSITY
Arthur Rense Prize
Donor: Paige Rense Noland

OKLAHOMA STATE UNIVERSITY
Academy of American Poets Prize
Donor: Oklahoma State University

OLD DOMINION UNIVERSITY
Academy of American Poets Prize
Donor: Carolyn Kreiter-Foronda

OREGON STATE UNIVERSITY
Weaver Undergraduate Poetry Award
Donor: Roger Weaver

PACE UNIVERSITY
David A. Bickimer Promise of Learnings
Poetry Prize
Donor: David Kermani

PENNSYLVANIA STATE UNIVERSITY
Leonard Steinberg Memorial Prize
Donor: Pearl Steinberg

PORTLAND STATE UNIVERSITY
English Award / Academy of
American Poets Prize
Donor: The Portland State University
Foundation

PRATT INSTITUTE
Academy of American Poets Prize
Donor: Pratt Institute

PRINCETON UNIVERSITY
Academy of American Poets Prize
Donor: William F. and Jerene Hewitt

PURDUE UNIVERSITY
Thomas H. Scholl and Elizabeth Boyd
Thompson Poetry Prize
Donor: Thomas H. Scholl

RANDOLPH-MACON WOMAN'S COLLEGE
Charles & Fanny Fay Wood Poetry Prize
Donor: Stephanie French

REED COLLEGE
President and Dean's Academy of
American Poets Prize

RHODE ISLAND SCHOOL OF DESIGN
Academy of American Poets Prize
Donor: Roger and Gayle Mandle

RICE UNIVERSITY
Academy of American Poets Prize
Donor: Joyce Pounds Hardy

ROCKFORD COLLEGE
Colleen Holmbeck Poetry Prize
Donor: Mary Weaks-Baxter

ROLLINS COLLEGE
Arden Goettling / Academy of
American Poets Prize
Donor: Family & Friends of Arden
Goettling

RUTGERS UNIVERSITY
Enid Dame Memorial Poetry Prize
Donor: Jeanne Marie Beaumont

ST. JOHN'S UNIVERSITY
Academy of American Poets Prize
Donor: Thomas McInerney

ST. LAWRENCE UNIVERSITY
James Ligon Price III Memorial Prize in
Poetry
Donor: St. Lawrence University

SAINT MARY'S COLLEGE OF CALIFORNIA
Russell & Yvonne Lannan Poetry Prize
Donor: John J. Lannan

ST. PETER'S COLLEGE
In Memoriam Gerald Kernan, S.J.,
Poetry Prize
Donor: James G. Butler

SAM HOUSTON STATE UNIVERSITY
The William C. Weathers Memorial Prize
Donor: Melissa Morphew

SAN FRANCISCO STATE UNIVERSITY
Harold Taylor Prize
Donor: The New Hope Foundation

SAN FRANCISCO STATE UNIVERSITY
(UNDERGRADUATE)
Academy of American Poets Piri Thomas
Poetry Prize
Donors: Friends and Family of Piri Thomas

SAN JOSE STATE UNIVERSITY
Virginia de Araujo Prize
Donor: Gloria Collins

SANTA CLARA UNIVERSITY
Tamara Verga Poetry Prize
Donor: Victoria Verga Logan

SARAH LAWRENCE COLLEGE (GRADUATE)
The John B. Santoianni Award For
Excellence in Poetry
Donors: Charmaine Ferenczi & Joseph
McCrindle

SARAH LAWRENCE COLLEGE
(UNDERGRADUATE)
Harold Taylor Prize
Donor: The New Hope Foundation

SHIMER COLLEGE
Ruth Cooley Poetry Prize
Donor: Peter Cooley

SINTE GLESKA UNIVERSITY
Stanley Red Bird Poetry Prize
Donor: J. Patrick Lannan

SKIDMORE COLLEGE
Academy of American Poets Prize
Donor: Skidmore College English
Department

SMITH COLLEGE
Anne Bradstreet Prize
Donor: Smith College

SOUTHERN ILLINOIS UNIVERSITY AT
CARBONDALE
Academy of American Poets Prize
Donor: Carolyn Forman Moe

SOUTHERN ILLINOIS UNIVERSITY AT
CARBONDALE (UNDERGRADUATE)
Academy of American Poets Prize
Donor: Rodney Jones

SPELMAN COLLEGE
Edith A. Hambie Poetry Prize
Donor: Anonymous

SPRING HILL COLLEGE
Reverend Andrew C. Smith, S.J., Poetry Prize
Donor: Lawrence Lannan

STANFORD UNIVERSITY
Academy of American Poets Prize
Donor: Kathleen Welton

STETSON UNIVERSITY
Holly M. Kimball Poetry Prize
Donor: Phillip Blumberg

SUNY ALBANY
Phyllis Hurd Liston Poetry Prize
Donor: Heather Liston

SUNY BINGHAMTON
Academy of American Poets Prize
Donor: SUNY Binghamton

SUNY BUFFALO
Friends of the University Libraries Prize
Donor: Sharon Schiffhauer

SUNY FARMINGDALE
Raynor Wallace Poetry Award
Donor: SUNY Farmingdale

SUNY OSWEGO
Academy of American Poets Prize
Donor: John W. Mincher, Jr.

SUNY PURCHASE
Friends of Humanities Poetry Prize
Donor: The SUNY Purchase Friends of
Humanities

SWEET BRIAR COLLEGE
Jean Taylor Meyer Memorial Poetry Prize
Donor: Jean Meyer Aloe

TEMPLE UNIVERSITY
Albert J. Caplan Prize
Donor: Albert J. Caplan

TRINITY COLLEGE
Academy of American Poets Prize
Donor: J. Ronald Spencer

TUFTS UNIVERSITY
Academy of American Poets Prize
Donor: Tufts University

TULANE UNIVERSITY
Anselle M. Larson / Academy of
American Poets Prize
Donor: Herbert V. Larson

UNION COLLEGE
Academy of American Poets Prize
Donor: Paul J. Boor

UNITED STATES NAVAL ACADEMY
Stuart Pitt Memorial Poetry Prize
Donor: A. Stuart Pitt

UNIVERSITY OF ALABAMA
Hill-Kohn Prize
Donor: University of Alabama English
Department

UNIVERSITY OF ALASKA, FAIRBANKS
Harold McCracken Endowment Poetry
Contest
Donor: Harold McCracken

UNIVERSITY OF ARIZONA
Academy of American Poets Prize
Donor: University of Arizona

UNIVERSITY OF CALIFORNIA, BERKELEY
Harold Taylor Prize
Donor: The New Hope Foundation

UNIVERSITY OF CALIFORNIA, DAVIS
Celeste Turner Wright Poetry Prize
Donor: Celeste Turner Wright

UNIVERSITY OF CALIFORNIA, IRVINE
Academy of American Poets Prize
Donor: Walter J. Thomson

UNIVERSITY OF CALIFORNIA,
LOS ANGELES
Fred and Edith Herman Memorial Prize
Donor: Joan LaBombard

UNIVERSITY OF CINCINNATI
(GRADUATE)
Academy of American Poets Prize
Donor: The George Elliston Poetry
Foundation

UNIVERSITY OF CINCINNATI
(UNDERGRADUATE)
Academy of American Poets Prize
Donor: The George Elliston Poetry
Foundation

UNIVERSITY OF DELAWARE
Harold Taylor Prize
Donor: The New Hope Foundation

UNIVERSITY OF DENVER
Edward M. Lannan Poetry Prize
Donor: John R. Lannan

UNIVERSITY OF HAWAI'I AT MANOA
Harold Taylor Prize
Donor: The New Hope Foundation

UNIVERSITY OF HOUSTON
Brazos Bookstore / Academy of American
Poets Prize
Donor: Karl Kilian

UNIVERSITY OF IDAHO
Academy of American Poets Prize
Donors: Karen Trujillo and Don Burnett

UNIVERSITY OF ILLINOIS AT
URBANA-CHAMPAIGN
Ruth Llewellyn Baird Prize
Donor: Robert D. Wood

UNIVERSITY OF IOWA WRITERS'
WORKSHOP
Harold Taylor Prize
Donor: The New Hope Foundation

University of Kansas
Ana Damjanov Poetry Prize
Donor: Ivan Damjanov

University of Mary Washington
Academy of American Poets Prize
Donor: Carolyn Kreiter-Foronda

University of Maryland
Prize in Memory of Anaïs Nin
Donor: Robert W. Newcomb

University of Massachusetts, Amherst
Academy of American Poets Prize
Donor: Donna Johnson

University of Massachusetts, Boston
Harold Taylor Prize
Donor: The New Hope Foundation

University of Memphis
Deborah L. Talbot Poetry Award
Donor: Deborah Talbot

University of Miami
Alfred Boas Poetry Prize
Donor: University of Miami

University of Michigan (Graduate)
Academy of American Poets Prize
Donor: Mrs. Sharon A. Galley

University of Michigan (Undergraduate)
Academy of American Poets Prize
Donor: Mrs. Sharon A. Galley

University of Minnesota
James Wright Prize for Poetry
Donor: University of Minnesota

University of Missouri at Columbia
Academy of American Poets Prize
Donor: Dottie Long

University of Montana
Academy of American Poets Prize
Donor: University of Montana

University of Nebraska, Lincoln
Wilbur Gaffney Poetry Prize
Donor: Professor Emeritus Wilbur Gaffney

University of Nebraska
Helen W. Kenefick Poetry Prize
Donor: John C. Kenefick

University of New Mexico
Academy of American Poets Prize
Donor: University of New Mexico

University of New Orleans
Andrea Saunders Gereighty Poetry Award
Donor: Andrea Gereighty

University of North Carolina at Chapel Hill
The Ann Williams Burrus Prize in Poetry
Donor: Ann W. Burrus

University of North Carolina at Greensboro
Noel Callow Poetry Award
Donor: H. T. Kirby-Smith

University of North Dakota
Thomas McGrath Award
Donor: University of North Dakota

University of Notre Dame
The Billy Maich Award
Donor: Jessica Maich

University of Pennsylvania
William Carlos Williams Prize
Donor: University of Pennsylvania

University of Pittsburgh
Academy of American Poets Prize
Donor: University of Pittsburgh

University of Redlands
Jean Burden Award
Donor: Virginia Everett Smith

University of Rhode Island
Academy of American Poets Prize
Donor: Ms. Nancy Potter

University of Richmond
Academy of American Poets Prize
Donor: Carolyn Kreiter-Foronda

University of Rochester
Marion Devendorf Van Laak Poetry Prize
Donor: The University of Rochester

University of San Francisco
Academy of American Poets Prize
Donor: University of San Francisco

University of Texas at Austin
Andrew Julius Gutow Poetry Prize
Donor: Stephen Gutow

University of the Arts
Sylvia B. Caplan Memorial Award
Donor: Albert J. Caplan

University of Utah
Craig Arnold Memorial Poetry Prize
Donor: University of Utah

University of Vermont
Ora Mary Pelham Poetry Prize
Donor: Sharon Lannan Ferrill

University of Virginia
Academy of American Poets Prize
Donors: English Dept., Henry Hoyns Bequest, Charles Wright

University of Washington
Harold Taylor Prize
Donor: The New Hope Foundation

University of Wisconsin, Madison
The Jens Bjerregaard Poetry Prize
Donor: Kevin P. Bjerregaard

University of Wisconsin, Milwaukee
Edward W. Ryan Poetry Prize
Donor: Mary Ann Ryan

Valdosta State University
Academy of American Poets Prize
Donor: Mr. Edward Davin Vickers

Valparaiso University
Vivian S. Richards Memorial Prize
Donors: Nancy & Michael Becker

Vanderbilt University
Academy of American Poets Prize
Donor: Madeleine J. Goodman

Vassar College
Mary Rousmaniere Gordon Prize
Donor: Albert Gordon

Virginia Commonwealth University
Catherine and Joan Byrne Poetry Prize
Donor: Nan Byrne

Virginia Polytechnic Institute
Virginia Tech / Poetry Society of Virginia Poetry Prize
Donor: Carolyn Kreiter-Foronda

Wartburg College
THE CASTLE Editor's Poetry Prize
Donor: Wartburg College

Washington & Lee University
Academy of American Poets Prize
Donor: Anonymous

Washington University
Academy of American Poets Prize
Donor: Washington University

Wayne State University
John Clare Prize
Donors: Nancy & Mr. Michael Becker

Wellesley College
Nevin Prize
Donor: Arthur W. Wadsworth

Wells College
Catharine B. De Pau Poetry Prize
Donor: Robert D. Corrie

Wesleyan College
George Warren Gignilliat, Jr. Poetry Prize
Donor: J. Edward Lantz

Wesleyan University
Sarah Hannah Memorial Prize
Donor: Kate Bernheimer

Westminster College
Anne Newman Sutton Weeks Prize
Donor: Westminster College

Wichita State University
Wichita State University Poetry Prize
Donor: Wichita State University

Williams College
Bullock Poetry Prize
Donor: Academy of American Poets

Yale University
Sean T. Lannan Poetry Prize
Donor: John R. Lannan

Academy of American Poets

The Academy of American Poets was founded in 1934 to support American poets at all stages of their careers and to foster the appreciation of contemporary poetry. To fulfill this mission, the Academy administers a wide variety of programs, including National Poetry Month (April), the largest literary celebration in the world; the Poetry Audio Archive, a collection of hundreds of recordings made over nearly five decades; an annual series of readings and events, including the Poets Forum; and Poets.org, our award-winning website, which provides a wealth of free content on contemporary poetry and receives a million visitors each month. The Academy also conducts High School Poetry Workshops and publishes the biannual journal, *American Poet*. In addition, the Academy administers the most important collection of poetry awards in the United States. These awards include the Wallace Stevens Award, the Academy Fellowship, the Lenore Marshall Poetry Prize, the James Laughlin Award, the Walt Whitman Award, the Raiziss/de Palchi Translation Award, the Harold Morton Landon Translation Award, and student prizes at more than 200 colleges and universities nationwide.

ABOUT THE UNIVERSITY & COLLEGE PRIZES

In 1955, the Academy of American Poets established its University & College Poetry Prize program at ten schools. The Academy now sponsors more than 200 annual prizes for poetry at colleges and universities nationwide, and has awarded more than $350,000 to nearly 10,000 student poets since the program's inception.

Many of America's most esteemed poets won their first recognition through the College Prize program, including Diane Ackerman, Toi Derricotte, Mark Doty, Alice Fulton, Tess Gallagher, Louise Glück, Allen Grossman, Jorie Graham, Kimiko Hahn, Joy Harjo, Robert Hass, Li-Young Lee, Brad Leithauser, J.D. McClatchy, Heather McHugh, Gregory Orr, Robert Pinsky, Sylvia Plath, Mark Rudman, Mary Jo Salter, George Starbuck, Mark Strand, and Charles Wright.

Establishing a Prize

The majority of the active University & College Prizes are endowed in perpetuity. The remainder are funded by special arrangement with the schools or donors. New schools are admitted into the program only with a $2,500 endowment contribution, which allows a prize of $100 (or two prizes totaling that amount) to be awarded each year, with additional interest applied toward the administrative costs of the program. We encourage anyone wishing to endow a college prize to contact the Academy's Awards Coordinator at (212) 274-0343 before selecting a school, as some of our oldest prizes do not yet have endowments, and we would very much like to see them secured for the future. A prize may be named by the donor or donors, and all contributions are fully tax-deductible. Donors receive copies of their schools' winning poems each year, as well as a lifetime subscription to *American Poet*, the Academy's biannual journal. A list of each year's winners is included in the Academy's Annual Report, and the Academy periodically publishes an anthology of selected prize-winning poems.